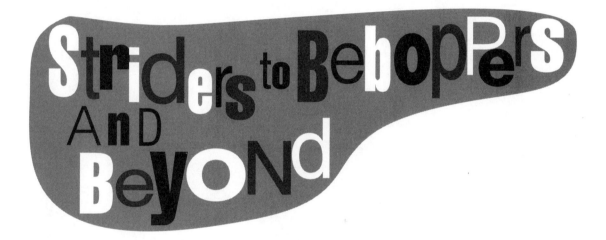

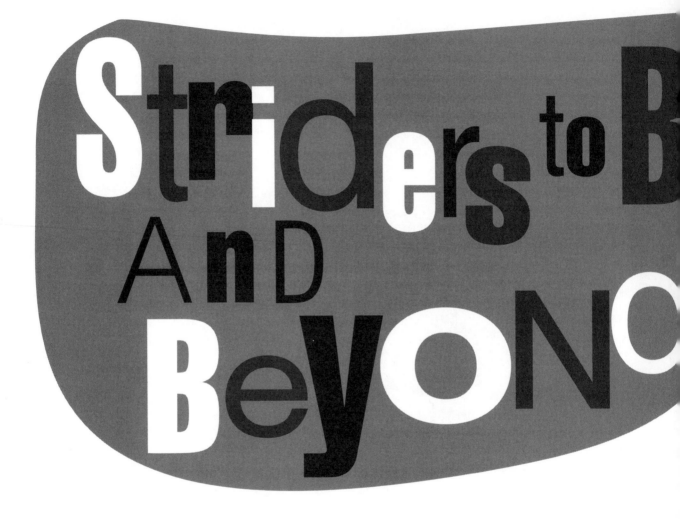

eboppers

The Art of Jazz Piano

Leslie Gourse

Franklin Watts

A Division of Grolier Publishing
New York / London / Hong Kong / Sydney
Danbury, Connecticut

Designed by John D. Sparks

Photos ©: Archive Photos: 75, 83 top (Metronome Collection), 81 top; Corbis-Bettmann: 83 bottom, 86, 90; Daniel Miller: 94 bottom (courtesy of Leslie Gourse); Frank Driggs Collection: 18, 24, 37, 42, 80, 87; Library of Congress: 15, 70; Retna Ltd: 65 (William P. Gottlieb), 92 (Dennis Kleiman), 91 (Veryl Oakland), 89, 94 top, 96 (David Redfern), 93 (Frans Schellekens); UPI/Corbis-Bettmann: 49, 109; William P. Gottlieb, Library of Congress: Ira & Leonore S. Gershwin Fund: 81 bottom, 82, 84.

Library of Congress Cataloging-in-Publication Data

Gourse, Leslie.
Striders to Beboppers and Beyond: The Art of Jazz Piano / by Leslie Gourse.

p.   cm. — (The Art of Jazz)
"Suggested listening": p.
Includes bibliographical references (p.) and index.
Summary: Describes the lives and artistry of some of the best-known jazz pianists, traces their influence on one another, and investigates the impact of different innovators on the development of jazz music.
ISBN 0–531–11320–5 (lib. bdg.)   0-531-15836-5 (pbk.)
1. Pianists—Biography—Juvenile literature. 2. Jazz musicians—Biography—Juvenile literature. [1. Pianists. 2. Musicians. 3. Jazz.]   I. Title.   II. Series.
ML3929.G68   1997
786.2'165'0922—dc20
[B]   96–31530
                                                                          CIP
                                                                      AC MN

ContENts

IntrODuction

The art of jazz piano, which began to develop around 1900, had two unique, vital characteristics. First: all jazz musicians, including pianists, accented the weak beat in a measure of music; this technique produced syncopation and swinging, danceable rhythms. Second, the music sounded spontaneous, as if it had been composed on the spur of the moment. That's because musicians improvised notes and phrases, embellishing the melodies and harmonies of songs. Improvisation was as important a part of jazz as its swinging rhythms. Each pianist used his or her imagination to improvise and express an individualistic personality.

Nearing the year 2000, musicians have developed jazz so much by improvising and experimenting that it barely resembles the loping, swinging music of a hundred years ago. All jazz players still have to improvise, but some music now called jazz has no trace of swing.

Striders to Beboppers and Beyond

Some jazz lovers argue among themselves about whether music can be called jazz if it doesn't at least imply a swinging pulse. The infectious, exciting rhythms not only made jazz famous but also influenced pop and classical composers all around the world. Duke Ellington, one of the greatest jazz pianists, orchestra leaders, and composers who ever lived, said: "It don't mean a thing if it ain't got that swing." Improvised music that doesn't swing at all might more correctly be called "new music."

No one has ever given a definition of jazz that everybody agrees with. Jazz experts now say, however, that music without the traditional rhythmic pulse can be called jazz if the music meets the crucial test of being improvised. A great deal of modern jazz composed at the end of the twentieth century still swings anyway. And for most jazz lovers, the word "jazz" still signifies improvised music played with at least some trace of the dance rhythm that made its early fans want to pat their feet on the floor.

Jazz has been played on nearly every kind of instrument. One of the crucial ones is the piano. It doesn't always create the most fanfare; that's often for the trumpet to do. It doesn't always sound as smoky as the saxophone. And it may not often be as fiery or throbbing as the drums. But the piano has royal status because of its capacity to let a good pianist play melody, harmony, and rhythm all at once.

- *The melody* is the familiar tune you hum after hearing a song.

- *Harmony* resides in the chords which support the melody; it sometimes even governs what the melody sounds like.

- *Rhythm* constitutes the beat and the tempo at which a piece of music is played.

Together, and even separately, melody, harmony, and rhythm create moods and communicate ideas to listeners.

Pianists sometimes regard themselves as orchestrators, because, with their ability to play melody, harmony, and rhythm at the same time, and with ten fingers which can play many notes at once, they can simulate the sound of an entire orchestra even when they are playing solo. A pianist who plays this way is said to have an orchestral approach.

People call the piano a percussion instrument because of the way the notes are produced. A pianist strikes a key, and this causes a felt hammer inside the instrument to strike a string. A pianist can reach inside and pluck strings, too. The piano can be played softly or loudly. And it has foot pedals that affect the overall sound, such as the loudness or clarity or brilliance of a note or the length of time it is held.

The piano is excellent for achieving a bittersweet, blues tonality; that tonality comes from flatted thirds, fifths, and sevenths. (A European music scale, which always has eight notes, can begin on any note. If a pianist plays the third, fifth, and seventh notes of any scale a half step down from the note that would constitute a whole step, the pianist is playing a flatted note in a blues scale, with the poignant tonality.)

Just about the only thing a pianist cannot do is play notes called microtones. If they were built into the instrument, they would be located between the eighty-eight existing keys. But microtones do not exist on pianos. To make up for the absence of extra keys, pianists can simultaneously or nearly simultaneously play two notes that are side by side. Then the piano can produce the slurred and vibrato-like sounds that wind instruments and the human voice can make.

That slurred sound is so important in jazz that it's one of the major hallmarks of the style. Slurred notes originated in gospel music sung in African-American churches and the blues derived from church music. Jazz gets some of its soulful, warm, personal feeling from slurred notes.

The piano, despite its lack of microtones, can produce a great variety of sounds. It is ideal for talented jazz musicians to play swinging rhythms and improvise melodies and harmonies. The excitement and virtuosity with which jazz pianists improvise determine their status as artists. An amateur pianist may know how to play a blues song. But Mary Lou Williams, who was one of the best and most visionary jazz pianists, composers, and arrangers, knew exactly how to play the whole piano, from its tinkling treble to its reverberating bass, and to use all its subtleties and strengths to make a blues song sound important and emotionally affecting.

Some of the best-known jazz pianists have been admired most of all for their virtuosity. Others have won fame for their innovative ideas and unique approaches to their instrument. Both virtuosos and inventors have had a mighty influence on the techniques of other players. Some pianists, such as Count Basie, became famous in the 1930s for playing soft, one-note melody lines. In the 1940s, Thelonious Sphere Monk, a great composer as well as a pianist, emphasized unusual harmonies above all. The way he sometimes stabbed his dissonant chords, with hesitating rhythms, gave him the most unorthodox style in jazz piano history. And McCoy Tyner, who became prominent in the 1960s, plays so many notes that his sound is dense, loud, and extremely dramatic. Critics have said that McCoy, like saxophonist John Coltrane, the most important group leader McCoy ever worked for, plays "sheets of sound."[1]

Jazz pianists have always studied the innovations that eventually become traditions. Pianists establish their own styles by expressing those traditions along with their own feelings and ideas, with their individual touches on the keys. Some have very delicate touches, such as John Lewis, the pianist in the Modern Jazz Quartet, who had a great deal of classical training. Others have had forceful approaches. Thelonious Monk played with his fingers flat on the keys—a technique that produced a heavy-handed sound. Kenny Barron, who likes to play long, flowing lines, has a light, firm touch.

Classical pianists learn exactly what notes to play and how to play them; there's only one correct way to play a piece of European classical music. The goal of the classical players is to interpret, not to reinvent, embellish, or improvise. Jazz pianists find no fixed routes to take. Many contemporary players abandoned classical studies precisely because they wanted to improvise. The excitement of jazz comes from the adventure of self-expression.

A Note about the Blues and the American Song Form

Most music played by traditional jazz pianists is written either in the blues or American song form. The blues form, which is so important to jazz, is usually a regular, twelve-measure song (though the number of measures can vary). Each group of four beats is called a measure or a bar, and each group of twelve measures or bars is called a chorus. Most people think a blues must be slow or moody. But that isn't necessarily so. You cannot always tell a blues by its sound. The old song, "Blues in the Night," is a moody-sounding twelve-bar blues. The popular rock song, "Rock Around the Clock," has the same form. Ray Charles's soul-rock music song, "What I Say," is another twelve-bar blues. The basic blues form is simple, but it can appear in many guises.

A musician can sing or play a blues in any key. In the key of C, the C chord starts the song for four bars; then the F chord goes on for two more bars; then the C chord sets up two bars; the G-seventh chord sets up the next two bars, and the C chord is used again for the last two bars. The ninth and tenth bars set up tension, and the eleventh and twelfth bars provide the resolution of the tension. The whole thing is called a blues chorus.

The American song form, which is derived from European music, has four sections. Each section is eight bars or measures long. A song has a total of thirty-two bars. If we use the letters A and B to signify each eight-bar section, we come up with the following plan: AABA. The B section is called the bridge, and it contains different material from the A section.[2]

Nobody has to know if a tune is written in blues or American song form to appreciate jazz. But anyone who wants to play jazz must know both forms very well.

CHAPTER ONE
Early Jazz
PiAniSts

The earliest form of jazz was a syncopated, two-beat music which had the feeling of march music. The left hand played an even beat, but the right hand played a syncopated rhythm — a ragged beat. So it was called ragtime. Ragtime combined European-influenced melodies and harmonies with syncopated, African-derived rhythms. Happy-sounding ragtime was the most popular music in the country from about 1900 to 1918. One of the greatest composers of rags was an African-American, Scott Joplin. He was born in Texas in 1868, a few years after slavery was ended. By 1899, he was living in Sedalia, Missouri, where he learned to write music formally, and where he published "Maple Leaf Rag," his most famous composition.

"Maple Leaf Rag" was named for a saloon in Sedalia where Joplin played piano. Most rags were performed in such places, never in concert halls. The flashier a ragtime pianist's technique, the more his audiences liked it. Many ragtime pianists had more entertaining stage presences than the shy, serious Scott Joplin. The best rag players earned the nickname "professor."[1] When rags were new to the world, the pianists usually performed them exactly the way they were written, with their clearly defined notes. Their music didn't necessarily have any relation to the soulful feeling of the blues, with its slurred notes and melancholy tone.

Other pianists, particularly in New Orleans, Louisiana, and New York City, did not confine themselves to playing rags. Syncopation, which stresses the weak beat in a musical measure, remained at the root of their rhythmic ideas, but they played and wrote a variety of song styles. Their repertoires included rags, European and ethnic music, the blues, American popular songs, musical theater songs, and church hymns and spirituals. And these pianists improvised.

One of the best known early pianists was New Orleans-born Ferdinand LeMenthe Jr., who developed his drawled, flowing, swinging style by loosening ragtime's rhythms and paring down its decorations. He started his career in barrooms, dance halls, honky-tonks, and brothels in New Orleans, and became famous in the early jazz world with the name Jelly Roll Morton.

Most people came to believe that trumpeter Louis Armstrong created the foundation of modern jazz. But Jelly Roll Morton claimed to have done it himself. It's true that some of Jelly Roll's ideas and accomplishments paralleled Armstrong's in the early years of the century. Both men listened to all the music around them—the blues, the rhythms of popular dances, Caribbean rhythms, Indian chants, Cajun songs, church music, and European classical music—and took inspiration to create their own fresh styles. Jelly Roll, who was born around 1885, was playing his earthy jazz in Storyville, the African-American section of New Orleans, by 1902. Louis Armstrong was only one year old then.

Jelly Roll was a Creole, meaning he had both African and white, particularly French, ancestry. He was a very light-skinned "man of color," as

Striders to Beboppers and Beyond

Creoles were described. He claimed to have been educated in both classical piano and opera, and he did hear performances of both. But as an orphaned teenager he became employed as a pianist in a brothel. He grew up at a time when the race lines were being drawn more sharply in New Orleans. Toward the end of the nineteenth century, the social, legal, and educational privileges of living as "people of color"[2] were taken away from Creoles. They became subject to the rigid segregation laws applied to African-Americans, people of primarily African ancestry.

As an adolescent, Jelly Roll had no choice as a professional musician except to play the music popular with African-Americans in New Orleans. The classical music world closed its doors to him. His grandmother was so angry about his lifestyle that she locked him out of the house. Not only was he a musician, but he became a pool hustler and a pimp, who lived by his wits in the crime-ridden red-light district of New Orleans. After the infamous nightlife of Storyville was shut down by the United States Department of the Navy in 1917, Jelly Roll wandered the country, seeking his fortune. Other musicians, too, left town and spread the sound of early jazz. By the early 1920s, Jelly Roll landed in Chicago, where he formed a band, the Red Hot Peppers. For the band, he wrote and recorded music with the happy, colorful, two-beat sound of New Orleans jazz.

Other musicians, including trumpeter Louis Armstrong, who went to Chicago in 1922, played some of Jelly Roll's songs. People may not always know the titles of his tunes anymore, but some of his melodies are still familiar, especially "King Porter Stomp" and "Jelly Roll Blues." Jelly Roll also recorded a well-known version of "Tiger Rag." He was never anywhere near as great a player on piano as Armstrong was on trumpet. But Jelly Roll had inventiveness and showmanship. He wrote careful arrangements with the exact notes for his band to play. In his solos, he seemed to have horn-like lines. He also paid great attention to his image and clothes; he even wore a diamond framed in gold in one of his front teeth.

Sedalia, Missouri: Scott Joplin wrote his famous rags here.

Striders to Beboppers and Beyond

Jelly Roll and many of the early jazz pianists often played solo; in New Orleans, bands were popular. Marching bands were hired to play dirges for funerals on the way to cemeteries. When they struck up a happy, syncopated hymn such as "Nearer My God to Thee" and headed home after a burial, the bands were joined by other musicians and dancers. These unpaid celebrants were called the Second Line. Other bands played for parties that took place every weekend on the shore of New Orleans's Lake Pontchartrain. Still other bands traveled on trucks around the city. And vocal quartets, some with an instrument or two, performed on the sidewalks. None of these groups had a pianist for the obvious reason: a musician can't carry a piano through the streets! So, in New Orleans, pianists played on their own in joints of all kinds.

Pianists could, of course, play with groups in clubs. As soloists, though, they could practically do the job of a whole band, if they approached the piano in an orchestral way—that is, if they regarded the piano as an orchestra and used the instrument to its full capacity. A pianist could play melody with variations in the right hand, while the left hand functioned as a rhythm section, playing rhythm and harmony. And one pianist was less expensive than an entire band. Jelly Roll said his first job as a pianist in a brothel paid him a dollar a night—plus tips. On his first night he earned twenty dollars in tips.[3] Later on, he would brag about earning much more.

Pianists as popular soloists were not confined to New Orleans's nightlife. In Baltimore, Maryland, for example, another pianist, Eubie Blake, began his career by playing in a brothel before the turn of the century. A few years older than Jelly Roll, Eubie, too, was very ambitious. And he was sufficiently committed to music to study it throughout his life. Eubie moved to New York City. By 1915, he began collaborating with an African-American lyricist named Noble Sissle.

Their tunes for popular shows appealed to both African-American and white audiences. Among their hits were "I'm Just Wild About Harry," "I'd Give a Nickel for a Dime," and "Memories of You." Their shows, such as *Hot Chocolates* and *Shuffle Along*, went from Harlem to

Broadway, and toured the United States and Europe in the 1920s and 1930s. Blake's career ended in the 1930s. The simple pop tunes he was composing had been trendy for a decade. Then the swing era began, and dance bands with nine instruments and more ruled the pop music world. Some pianists found jobs as members of those bands. Eubie Blake didn't belong in that world.

He was forgotten for decades in New York City, but he did not stay idle. He studied composition at New York University. Then, in 1969, he was invited to give a concert at the Newport Jazz Festival. His talents were rediscovered. At that time, solo piano was coming back into fashion. He remained active as a professional pianist, playing his repertoire, until he was ninety-nine years old. He was honored at the Kennedy Awards ceremony in Washington, D.C., where he heard the orchestra playing one of his songs. He liked it, but he couldn't remember if he had written it. "That's a pretty tune. Did I write it?" Blake asked singer Joe Williams. Joe, who was there to help with the celebration, assured him he had written it.[4] Eubie died from pneumonia five days after his hundredth birthday.

Many in the jazz world have had ups and downs like Eubie's. Some jazz pianists have had professional careers that spanned four or five decades and more. Some have found themselves in and out of the spotlight. Others developed in complexity to accept the challenges of changing times and fashions in jazz. And many jazz pianists have been so accomplished in a particular style that their artistry and influence have endured and remained popular despite new trends and advances in music.

Not only Jelly Roll and Eubie Blake but other African-American pianists in many cities in the early 1900s found jobs playing solo, usually in rough joints or at rent parties. People threw rent parties when they were unable to pay their rent: they barbecued chickens and boiled collard greens, invited their friends, and charged a small admission, usually twenty-five cents. They also hired a pianist, called a "tickler,"[5] to play all night for a few dollars or at least a share of the food and drinks.

Eubie Blake and Noble Sissle in the 1920s; they collaborated on popular musical shows in New York and toured with them.

Often several pianists showed up at these parties and tried to outplay each other. The guests loved the "cutting contests," as they were called.[6] Musicians in Harlem played in a style called stride piano. This was similar to the New Orleans style, but stride was faster and often brighter, with less of the underlying feeling of a dirge and more of a European and musical theater influence. Stride fit better with the faster-paced and more sophisticated life in New York.

Some stride pianists achieved lasting fame—among them James P. Johnson, Willie "the Lion" Smith, and Fats Waller. Because they composed and recorded a great deal, Johnson and Waller in particular have influenced generations of jazz pianists. Chicago was known more as a haven for blues musicians and boogie-woogie players with their intense, exciting, repetitive rhythmic style. But New York was the most popular city in the country for all the arts. And so Harlem and the stride style flowered in the 1920s.

In 1922, Joe Turner, a fifteen-year-old boy in Baltimore, set his sights on Harlem. His parents were church-going people who had been delighted when he started playing organ at age five. But when he went to work in a club, he recalled, "I became the black sheep because I messed with jazz. My parents wanted me to become a preacher or a lawyer."[7]

Musicians passing through town boosted his self-esteem by telling him he was a "child wonder." That was enough to convince him to try his luck in Harlem. "I told my mother a lie that I had a job. Well, I didn't have a job, but I had plenty courage. I also had $1.20 left over in my pocket after the train fare when I got to New York. I asked around about where the colored people were. Harlem, they told me. So I went to Harlem, carrying my pasteboard suitcase, and I got off the subway and asked where the musicians hung out. Somebody told me to go to the Comedy Club. I ate a 25-cent meal and walked around to see Harlem. That night I went with my suitcase to the Comedy Club." Turner called it the Comedy Club, but it may have been the Capitol Palace, where stride pianists congregated.

"When I got inside, I saw a piano, and different people would go up and play a couple of tunes. I asked if it was okay for me to play. The waiter said, 'Sure.' So I played 'Carolina Shout' and 'Harlem Strut' by James P. Johnson [these were two of Johnson's most famous songs]. I had learned them from pianola rolls in Baltimore by putting my fingers on the keys as they went down until I could play them myself." Pianola rolls were perforated strips of paper that transmitted the information necessary for a player piano to play a tune; they were very popular until juke boxes, phonographs, and radios became common. "Someone said, 'You're good, and there's the composer over there.' James P. Johnson was in the club. . . . I asked him to play those tunes. He obliged and commended my own playing."

Another member of the audience helped Joe get a place to live and a gig at Barron Wilkins's club on 134th Street in Harlem. Wilkins apologized for not being able to pay him more than thirty dollars a week. Joe had never earned more than twelve dollars a week. He thought: "They're crazy up in New York." He was very happy, because he met all the best stride players, and they befriended him. "If they hadn't, things wouldn't have gone very well for me, but I was lucky," Turner said. "James P. Johnson called it stride. . . . I guess it was because it's just like striding down the avenue when you play it. You have your own accompaniment, like the bass and guitar, going with your left hand, and the melody is improvised with your right hand."

Joe Turner found his first major job with saxophonist Benny Carter's orchestra for three years. When Carter left the band, Louis Armstrong took over, and Turner stayed on. When he was twenty-three, he accompanied Adelaide Hall, a well-known singer in Harlem, who had won praise for her part in the 1928 production of a popular musical series called *Blackbirds*. In 1930, she took him to play as her accompanist in England. During a side trip to Paris, he decided he wanted to live there. He was hired by a European orchestra. "I loved the social and artistic freedom so much," he said. Paris was not segregated. "I stayed until the war broke out in 1939, and then went back to the U.S. and into the Army."

After World War II, he moved to Europe and stayed for the rest of his life. Legendary American jazz players recorded with him there. He played from midnight to five A.M. at a fashionable club, Calvados, near the Champs-Élysées. And he always had a cigar in his mouth. On July 21, 1990, in his eighties, he died in Paris.

Harlem stride pianist Willie "the Lion" Smith, who also always had a cigar, was one of the best players in Harlem when Joe Turner arrived. Smith composed and recorded some songs such as "Echoes of Spring," and he preferred to stay up all night and play in clubs rather than make records. James P. Johnson, who did more recording, became known as a more important and prolific composer.

Stride pianists could play the entire spectrum of popular music, including the blues, in their own way. Blues pianists chugged along, playing the rocking blues rhythm with the left hand while the right hand roamed around in the middle and upper-middle registers of the piano. But stride pianists did not concentrate on that soulful, church-derived music in a traditional way. The left hand alternated between playing chords and distant, single, sharply sounded notes, making rapid strides between the chords and notes. The sleight of hand gave their music a great, proud bounce. The right hand played blues and ragtime variations, but also explored other musical ideas and brought European themes into the music. Stride players weren't well-schooled or classically-trained musicians, but they knew something of European classical and Impressionist music. The European influence gave stride players an airy, thoughtful, cultivated sound.

All the stride players had colorful personalities. They made the rounds of many clubs, including Barron Wilkins's, where Joe Turner had his first job, and the Capitol Palace, a downstairs nightclub where Duke Ellington and probably Count Basie, too, first heard Willie "the Lion" Smith play. Duke Ellington noticed that everyone in that club, even the waiters, moved to the hypnotic tempo at which "the Lion" played. Some people said Smith was the greatest stride player; others claimed Johnson was king. Still others thought a man named Luckey Roberts ranked as the best. Roberts left a small legacy on records, too. (A teenage pianist visiting New York in 1920, Earl Hines, would always remember that Roberts played with such power and fervor that he sent the keys of a worn-out piano flying around a room.) These were the kings of Harlem stride.

Willie "the Lion" Smith, born in Goshen, New York, in 1897 and raised in Newark, New Jersey, was self-taught in a family that loved music. He started playing in rough Newark clubs at age fourteen, learning techniques by ear from other players. In his late teens, he arrived in Harlem, where he became friends with the best piano players. At nineteen, he enlisted in the Army; he fought bravely with the infantry during World War I in France and then returned to Harlem. By then he had his nickname. He was a tall, swashbuckling figure who loved to socialize. And he could pound the piano aggressively. In Europe, he also learned to love the Impressionist players and composers Maurice Ravel and Claude Debussy. They tempered his sound with a romantic, refined quality.

In Harlem, Smith met James P. Johnson, who had been born in New Brunswick, New Jersey, in 1894. Johnson's parents liked to invite friends to their house, where Mrs. Johnson played piano. Guests sang and danced an old Southern "ring shout," a circling dance, with its roots in African ritual, that had been invented by slaves.[8] In America, it became part of the Baptist tradition and then was adapted for social occasions. When James P. Johnson's parents moved to Jersey City, he met his first "ticklers," whose lifestyles in clubs impressed him. Women swarmed around them. They dressed well. And their keyboard abilities assured them of their welcome everywhere.

When James P. was fourteen, his family moved to New York's tough midtown neighborhood, San Juan Hill, which bordered on Hell's Kitchen and the Tenderloin around 34th Street. In these neighborhoods, called "the Jungles,"[9] lived many poor people from all ethnic and racial backgrounds. James P. went to places in the Jungles where people played piano. At the same time, he was growing into a sensitive, mild-mannered young man who had little interest in the rawness of life and the fights in places where he played.

He began composing blues tunes, hoping he could publish them and escape from his sad environment. He also taught himself about the

European classical composers Bach and Beethoven and learned to notate his music from a musician he met on the scene. Johnson sold several original songs in 1915. But he had to keep playing in saloons, where he won prizes in contests. His reputation led to an invitation for him to record about twenty pianola rolls, most of them his own ragtime-based compositions. The music he had heard as a child continued to have the greatest influence on all his work as a composer.

He began fulfilling his dream of writing for musical theater when he became involved as a musical director for the show *Plantation Days* in 1922. Then he went on to the show *Runnin' Wild*. A dance number, "The Charleston," which he wrote for that show, contributed to the Charleston dance craze that spread around the country. (Eubie Blake also wrote a Charleston rag.) Johnson also wrote popular songs such as "If I Could Be with You One Hour Tonight" and "Carolina Shout." When the show *Runnin' Wild* became popular on Broadway, James P. Johnson reigned as the dean of Harlem piano players.

In those days, a chubby teenager, Thomas "Fats" Waller, followed him around. Johnson brought Waller to a cutting contest, for which Waller played "Carolina Shout" so well that Willie "the Lion" Smith also recognized the young protégé's ability. Waller had an exceptional spark in his sound. He was accepted as one of the three leading players in Harlem.

Fats's parents had migrated from Virginia to Greenwich Village in New York City in the 1880s; they moved uptown to San Juan Hill, then joined the first African-American families to move to Harlem. Fats was born there on May 21, 1904, one of five Waller children who survived childhood. (Six others died young.) Waller's mother was so overprotective that she rarely let her children out of the house. She particularly doted on Fats. When he did get out of the house, he was so thrilled to be on his own that he became a nonstop socializer. He would become as renowned among his friends for his appetites for food, liquor, and parties as for his music.

He had begun playing a piano in a neighbor's house when he was six. He also loved the way his mother, a soloist in the Abyssinian Baptist Church choir, sang the stirring hymns at home. His very strict father,

Fats Waller at the Yacht Club on 52nd Street in New York in the 1930s; Fats became renowned as a great stride style pianist and song composer.

Edward, a preacher, shifted the family to a Pentecostal church, where the exciting, thumping rhythms of the services had an enormous effect on young Fats. The Waller family acquired an upright piano for one of the girls to play, but Fats got lessons, too, because he was so talented.

His father did not approve of his son's interest in popular music. Yet when Fats was chosen to play piano for school events, his father was so proud that he took Fats to hear a great European classical pianist, Paderewski, play at Carnegie Hall. Fats appreciated Paderewski, but he loved ragtime, as it was still called, best of all. His parents called it "the devil's music." That was the attitude of many Christians in those times.

By age fourteen, already weighing about two hundred pounds, Fats had earned his nickname. He left school and went to work. Because his mother had become very ill, worn out by childbearing, he had little supervision and went wherever he wanted. Some of his jobs were connected to music, others to food and liquor; he delivered bottles of bootleg liquor hidden under his baggy clothing and also became a messenger for a delicatessen.

Soon Fats was playing a Wurlitzer pipe organ for silent movies at Harlem's Lincoln Theater. At first he "sat in"—played without pay—and substituted for the hired organist. His playing improved with regular work, and he went on the payroll. White people from the downtown Broadway world came up to hear the shows at the Lincoln.

His mother died in 1920. Waller moved to a friend's house, where he began studying the player piano in the parlor, fitting his fingers to the depressed keys as it rolled off the popular tunes of the day. That's how he learned the piano rolls. A friend introduced him to James P., who took the boy home to live with him and his sister. They had two pianos, which Johnson and Waller played together. James P. would later recall, "He picked up all the stomps and rags I knew and that walkin' bass, too. . . . I taught him how to groove, how to make it sweet. . . . He stuck pretty well to my pattern, developed a lovely swinging tone, a large melodic expression and, being the son of a preacher, he had fervor."[10]

Striders to Beboppers and Beyond

Johnson's sister recalled how Waller would play piano until the wee hours of the morning. "That walkin' bass" which James P. taught him—the left hand stride technique—was an element Fats had certainly not gotten from playing the organ. Johnson put Waller through scale exercises and taught him about melody in improvisation and the history of ragtime-based improvisations.

Fats married a young woman named Edith, whose family took him into their house but not into their hearts. They harassed him about his musical career and wanted him to find regular employment. Edith had been a polite dinner guest in Fats's house when his mother had been alive. Fats may have married Edith because she reminded him of those days. But Edith was the wrong wife for him. When they had their first baby, Thomas Jr., Fats went on a tour to earn more money. He came home to discover his wife was furious. She threatened him with divorce, locked him out, and began a long battle with him about alimony and child support.

By 1923, Waller made a very important professional connection. After winning a piano contest at the Roosevelt Theater in the early 1920s, he was chased down on the street by a budding lyricist, Andy Razaf. They went to a coffee shop and talked. Razaf was the organized, disciplined artist, Waller the untamed, carefree spirit. Together they wrote some of the best songs of their careers—romantic, spirited, blithe songs such as "Ain't Misbehavin," "Keepin' Out of Mischief," "Blue Turning Grey Over You," "Concentratin' on You," "Honeysuckle Rose," "The Joint Is Jumpin'," and the racial protest song "What Did I Do to Be So Black and Blue?" with which Louis Armstrong caused a stir in a Broadway theater in the 1920s. Together, with others, and individually, Waller and Razaf wrote many songs that musicians played for the rest of the century.

Waller developed into a tasteful, versatile pianist with a light, straight style influenced by musical theater, a commanding, rhythmic drive from stride and church music, and a sparkle from his own genius. He became a teacher and role model for budding musicians. William Basie, sojourn-

26

ing in Harlem before he became the legendary bandleader Count Basie, learned to play the organ by watching Waller in Harlem theaters. Then Waller gave lessons to Basie and even taught Basie to improvise music. Basie looked at the movie on the screen and played whatever came to his mind to enhance the emotion or action in the story. Learning his lessons well, Basie later held a job playing in a movie theater in Kansas City, Missouri, before he formed his first band there.

In 1931, Waller, whose conviviality led him to know every club and musician in Harlem, met a teenager named Art Tatum. Tatum, who was legally blind (his vision was very impaired), had arrived from Toledo, Ohio, to accompany the popular, highly-cultivated, pretty soprano Adelaide Hall. (Joe Turner was another of her accompanists.) After meeting Tatum backstage in a theater, Waller invited him to go drinking and club-hopping. Tatum loved that lifestyle, too. In one club, they found a piano, which Waller began to play. Tatum had to pick up the challenge and follow Fats. James P. Johnson was in the house and heard them play. Tatum's left hand complicated the stride rhythm, while his right hand played very difficult, light, swift, and extended improvisations guided by his genius for harmonies. The multitalented Waller recognized that he had met an even greater piano player in Tatum. Tatum filled all other pianists with awe; world famous classical pianists, who usually didn't listen to jazz musicians, would go to hear Tatum play.

One night in the mid-1930s, Waller was sitting in at the Onyx Club on West 52nd Street. Tatum, who loved to finish a job and then go to another place to play all night for pleasure, walked into the Onyx. Waller noticed him and told the audience, "Ladies and gentleman, I play piano, but God is in the house tonight!"[11] Tatum then sat down to play.

Both Tatum's hands were so swift that people couldn't keep track of which hand was playing what. He was a master of dazzling, bravura runs and fascinating harmonic adventures. His work was so ornate that people sometimes criticized him for decorating his music too much. That was the only criticism they could dream up. A well-known cornetist and jazz historian in the 1930s, Rex Stewart, wrote that Tatum used a hazelnut,[12] whose size he chose with great care, to run through his fingers to develop dexterity. When he wore out one hazelnut, he bought another. And he sat for hours practicing scales and exercises.

Born with cataracts, Art suffered through operations until sight was restored fairly well in one eye. Then, the legend is, he was robbed on the street by someone who hit him in his good eye and blinded him again. He continued playing, leading a trio with a bass and guitar in the 1940s, but his virtuosity overwhelmed his sidemen. His solo piano records are among the greatest in the jazz repertoire.

Blindness didn't stop Tatum from staying out all night to play piano. But Fats Waller's life was even more disorganized than Tatum's. For one of Waller's most famous songs, "Ain't Misbehavin'," Waller accepted a fifty-dollar payment, selling the rights for twenty years. He always needed money for alimony and child support for his first wife.

With his second wife and children, Waller was much happier. But he had voracious appetites for food and alcohol, and he weighed 285 pounds at one point in the 1930s. When he traveled, he always threw parties in hotel rooms. At home in Harlem, he always went to his favorite hangout, Connie's Inn. Though he became a star on records for Victor, his lifestyle kept him in debt. His talent kept him going; he could show up at a recording session without a rehearsal or written music and compose wonderful songs on the spot. But he wore himself out. On a train in 1943, returning from performances in California to his beloved Harlem, he became very ill one winter night. He died on that train, of pneumonia, at age thirty-nine.

In the 1990s, young pianists beginning to find commercial and artistic success in New York were often asked who their favorite pianists were. Many of them named Art Tatum for his virtuosity and Fats Waller "for the joy of his music."[13]

CHAPTER TWO
The DoMinant Pianists oF the SwiNg Era

While the stride players were holding court in Harlem, and blues players reigned in Chicago, a new trend in music was developing. People were becoming excited about big bands that played for dances. The bands had a wide variety of styles and sounds. Some were classified as hot and swinging, and others were sweet, smooth, and lilting. By 1934, a craze for big bands was sweeping the country. The big band era would last until about 1947.

Bands became popular for several reasons. First of all, Americans love bigness, and a band with thirteen instrumentalists or more playing upbeat music for dancing simply excited the public more than a soloist or a small band. Furthermore, new technology helped spread the sound of the big bands.

At first, musicians made acoustic recordings, playing into a megaphone. Record players, then called victrolas, also had megaphones through which the recordings were heard. By 1920, the carbon micro-phone was improving the quality of recordings. And electrical recording replaced acoustic recording by 1926. Carbon microphones and electrical recording improved the quality of sound so much that instruments which could barely be heard on acoustic recordings, such as the bass, came into wider use.

In 1920 or 1921, record producers discovered a good market for "race records,"[1] which were aimed at the African-American community and produced on a tight budget. The music of African-Americans as well as white musicians began to spread to all parts of the country.

Some of those "race records" by African-Americans were heard by white audiences and musicians, who borrowed from the style. At the same time, African-American musicians admired and learned from some of the white bands. Most of all, radio spread the sound of the big bands. When they played for dancing and dining in hotels, their music was broadcast live on radio shows called "remotes."[2]

Paving the way for the style of music played by big bands for their remotes, the success of the Original Dixieland Jazz Band focused atten-tion on this exciting music. That band of white musicians from New Orleans, who left town when the Navy closed Storyville, scored a big hit in a New York City club in 1917 and helped make jazz a household word. Cabarets everywhere featured little jazz bands. Another popular white group was the Mound City Blue Blowers from St. Louis. Its three amateur musicians played the banjo, comb, and kazoo. The Wolverines, a group with a legendary cornet player, Bix Beiderbecke, scored a big hit. So did the Austin High School Gang in Chicago. Beiderbecke, who eventually joined a famous big band led by Paul Whiteman, had a great influence on many musicians, and he inspired songwriters such as Hoagy Carmichael, the composer of "Stardust." Bands formed all around the country, some made up of white musicians, others of African-Americans.

As a young man, Paul Whiteman set out from San Francisco with his big band. In 1924, he presented a jazz concert aiming to play dance music in a jazzy fashion and to make the style respectable. He succeeded, and his publicists crowned him the King of Jazz.[3]

After World War I, African-Americans began migrating from the Deep South to the Southwest. Musicians found audiences in Texas, Oklahoma, Arkansas, Kansas, and Missouri. Though most people in the country knew only about white bands at this time, a regular touring circuit for African-American dance bands sprang up in the Southwest and Midwest.

By 1927, an African-American bandleader named Walter Page led his Blue Devils on a tour of the Southwest. Count Basie joined the band and, after Page died, led his own band based in Kansas City. Also in the 1920s, Andy Kirk brought his band, the Clouds of Joy, with a very young woman pianist and arranger, Mary Lou Williams, to Kansas City. Oklahoma-born pianist Jay McShann settled in Kansas City and began leading groups by the end of the 1930s. (He hired an alto saxophonist named Charlie "Bird" Parker, who would later influence all jazz musicians.)

During the Depression and Prohibition, when the banks failed and liquor was illegal, Kansas City became a center for jazz activity. The town's political boss, Tom Pendergast, kept the city wide open for gamblers, drinkers, and everyone else who loved nightlife. To heighten the excitement, club owners hired jazz bands to entertain the revelers. For a while, Kansas City rivaled New York City's importance in the development of jazz.

In Harlem in 1927, pianist Duke Ellington, who was creating his own eloquent, percussive style, took his band, with many great musicians who would remain with him for decades, into the glamorous Cotton Club. New York clubs and ballrooms attracted bands from all over the country. Those that broadcast from New York on radio networks cultivated fans everywhere. When the musicians went on the road, dancers came out in droves for their favorites. While in New York, African-American bands went to the Savoy Ballroom in Harlem to compete with each other. And all jazz musicians dreamed of going to New York—the Big Apple—to find fame and fortune.

Louis Armstrong, who had been playing with bands in Chicago in the early 1920s, was encouraged by his wife, pianist Lil Hardin, to travel to New York. There he played with Fletcher Henderson's band, one of the best early African-American bands. Henderson's arrangements were used by several admiring white bands. But most couldn't play the music the way Henderson's men did. It wasn't until 1934 that a white band-leader, clarinetist Benny Goodman, used the Henderson arrangements very successfully.

Earl Hines

After having the experience of playing with Fletcher Henderson, Louis Armstrong decided to go back to Chicago in 1925. When he did, he met a young pianist named Earl Hines. Working together, they established the highest standards yet achieved for modern jazz playing. Ever since, Hines has been called "Fatha" (for "father"), respected for establishing the foundation of the art of modern jazz piano playing.

He was also one of the most influential players from the late 1920s until the 1940s, when the bebop revolution and its players extended Hines's ideas virtually beyond recognition. But all pianists, from Hines's contemporaries—Ellington, Basie, Tatum, and two other very influential players of the 1930s, Mary Lou Williams and Teddy Wilson—to the beboppers, learned from Hines's ideas for playing jazz on the piano. He established new techniques both as a soloist and within an ensemble, and he inspired all other pianists to become more creative and develop their own styles.

In the big bands, pianists could no longer function as independent mavericks who played whatever and whenever they wanted to. They had to adapt to the needs of the bands. But basing their techniques on Hines's ideas, they could use the size and strength of a band and the piano's capacities to highlight the instrument in new ways. Some older musicians rued the decline of the popularity of solo stride piano. But big band pianists discovered they had more freedom than ever to explore the harmonies and melodies of songs and become greater improvisers, while bassists and drummers took over the work that had formerly been done by the left hands of stride pianists. A bassist, a guitarist, and a drummer played the rhythmic foundation of songs. Together with a pianist, they were called the rhythm section.

Also because of Hines, pianists found ways to adapt cannily to the dynamics—the loudness—of the big bands. With new techniques, pianists made themselves heard clearly, so they didn't get lost in the great roar of the hot, swinging bands.

Earl Hines was born on December 28, 1905, in Duquesne, near Pittsburgh, Pennsylvania. His father played cornet, his stepmother the organ; his mother's sister sang light opera, and his mother's uncle played all the brass instruments. His uncle was "a terrific musician," he recalled in his life story, *The World of Earl Hines*, told to Stanley Dance, a leading writer on the swing era.[4]

In the house, Earl started imitating his stepmother on the organ and overheard his father say, "Do you think he might like music?"[5] After taking a few lessons, he outstripped his first teacher. So he went to study with a strict German teacher. His father took him to hear music performances, where Earl learned songs by ear. By the time he was twelve, he was playing organ in the Baptist church the family attended. Though he found it hard to reach the pedals, he could play the music easily. He had already gone through books by Chopin and other European composers. In church, he earned three dollars a month, playing all day on Sundays for services and special programs. Soon he found out about opportunities to play in competitions in towns around Duquesne.

During his high school years, he lived with his aunt, the singer, and became friends with other budding musicians. One was a singer, a young man named Lois Deppe. In his aunt's house, Earl met Eubie Blake and Noble Sissle, who traveled with their shows, and Luckey Roberts, the

Striders to Beboppers and Beyond

Harlem stride player. When Earl was fifteen, his cousin and friends, who had jobs, took him to Pittsburgh nightclubs. The older boys were thrilled with the meals and the girls. Earl loved the music he heard.

Lois Deppe wanted to start a band with Earl as the pianist. Earl said he was too young. So Lois asked permission from Earl's father and aunt. The fifteen-year-old began to play for Lois during the summers at a club on Pittsburgh's busy Wylie Avenue. "That's where I really began to gain experience," Earl would recall about his two years at the club. He heard an intriguing pianist there who "didn't use his fifth finger but stretched his fourth finger to make tenths (with his left hand,) and this was the first time I had seen or heard of the tenths [two notes played with an interval of ten notes between them]. I found out that there was a lot of harmony and rhythm being carried as well as the bass."[6] Earl's hands were still too small to play tenths, but he learned to stretch his fingers, and after a while he could perform them. Using his salary of fifteen dollars a week, Earl bought beer and chewing tobacco to pay the impressive pianist to give him lessons and teach him to play "beautiful, soft piano."[7]

Another pianist dazzled Hines by playing tenths with his right hand. That pianist's hand was so large that he played the melody with his middle fingers and used his thumb and last finger for the tenths. This pianist also had great speed in his right hand. Earl could play fast because of his training, but he couldn't make the tenths for quite a while.

He also met a fine trumpeter, Joe Smith. Passing through town, Smith would go on to establish a good reputation with Blake and Sissle and then some early jazz bands. When Smith used a coconut shell for a mute, he got a velvet tone, Earl noticed. "I marveled at his style and wanted to play what he played on trumpet."[8]

Earl also liked other entertainers' stagecraft and clothes—silk shirts, gold jewelry, strong leather boot-like shoes, and even diamonds as decorations in their front teeth. For several years, Earl traveled around the Pittsburgh area with Lois Deppe. Once Earl earned sixty-five dollars for a single party. Another time, he was delighted to be the first African-

American pianist to play on the radio station KDKA in Pittsburgh. With Deppe, Earl learned how to accompany and coach singers.

Eubie Blake, passing through town several times, urged Earl to go to New York. But Earl was reluctant. For one thing, young as he was, he had fallen in love with and married a singer. Then he found out that his wife was running around with a man who traveled in fast company. A musician asked Earl to go to work in a band in a Chicago club. Earl's aunt promised she would send him money to get home if he ran into trouble. So in 1923, at age eighteen, he decided to gamble on his talent.

He found work right away in Chicago, playing from midnight to six A.M. in the Elite No. 2, an after-hours club. He became immersed in the jazz world and lifestyle of Chicago's African-American South Side around State Street and 135th Street. And he began to attract attention as a lanky boy playing piano with an unusual style.

A bandleader, Carroll Dickerson, who played violin, kept inviting Earl to join his band in a club. Earl joined shortly before the club closed. Then Dickerson took his band on the road for a long tour. Earl kept learning, sometimes the hard way, about the entertainment world and the ways of the world in general. Gambling too much, he spent one Christmas Eve with only enough money for a dinner of salted crackers. He found out about all the ways that discrimination could enforce segregation and keep him out of clubs, even when segregation wasn't the law.

With his quick wit, Earl learned how to negotiate his way through crises. Carroll Dickerson, for example, was such a heavy drinker that sometimes he lost his place in the music on stage. One night he was so muddled that he kept leading the band after the performance was finished. Earl noticed his boss's difficulty and played until Dickerson stopped. After the show, Dickerson said to Earl, "That was a nice thing you did."

The club's manager said, "Yes, it was. You saved the act."

"I kind of lost my place in the music," Dickerson said.

"No, it wasn't that," Earl said. "We shortened the arrangement and hadn't told you."[9]

Striders to Beboppers and Beyond

The band traveled for forty-two weeks during 1926 on the Pantages Circuit, a well-known theater circuit in those days, and went back to Chicago as a glamorous, seasoned group. The Sunset Café hired it, and Louis Armstrong, billed as the World's Greatest Trumpeter, became its lead trumpeter. Earl and Louis had already become friends when they met and played together in the musicians' union hall on State and 39th Street. "I knew right away that he was a giant,"[10] Hines said.

The band featuring Earl and Louis at the Sunset was exciting. All the musicians were talented—all could read music, in fact, which was unusual. The Sunset's floor show had excellent dancers and comedians, and the club was popular. Hines was able to make friends with influential nightlife people, gangsters included. So he stayed safe and developed his playing, though the section of town he worked in was dangerous. He saw at least two unpredictable characters get killed in a gunfight. Some people even fought with the police. Hines understood why Jelly Roll Morton, who was living in Chicago at the time, carried pearl-handled pistols and earned a reputation for being a loudmouth. "You had to act bad, whether you were bad or not,"[11] Hines observed. Staying out of fights, he paid attention to learning from the best bandleaders.

His boss, Carroll Dickerson, drank so much that the Sunset fired him. Louis Armstrong was appointed the leader, and Earl became the musical director. White musicians who would become legendary in jazz—Benny Goodman with his clarinet in a sack, Tommy Dorsey with his trombone and trumpet, Tommy's brother Jimmy Dorsey with his alto sax and clarinet, cornetist Muggsy Spanier, and pianist Jess Stacy—came to sit in with the group. So did Fats Waller, when he went to Chicago to play at the Vendome Theater. Hoagy Carmichael dropped in to play his composition "Stardust" on piano. It would become one of the most famous popular songs in the country.

Louis and Earl became inseparable friends. Earl wrote a song, "A Monday Date," as a reminder for Louis, who sometimes forgot to keep his dates with Earl. Musically the pianist and trumpeter inspired each other to new heights of creativity and rejoiced in playing music together.

Earl Hines (far left) played and recorded with Louis Armstrong's early great bands. Louis is fourth from the left in this 1927 picture of the Stompers at the Sunset Café.

Striders to Beboppers and Beyond

Hines would later say that he and Louis used each other's musical ideas freely. It was during their days at the Sunset Café that the Okeh Records company invited Louis to record. In 1927 and 1928, Hines became a member of Armstrong's Hot Five and Hot Seven Bands, studio groups for Okeh. Together, they recorded many immortal sides, including "West End Blues."

In 1928, Hines left Armstrong's band. Earl, Louis, and the drummer Zutty Singleton had made a pact to stick together after the Sunset Café closed. But times were lean. Earl went to New York for a short time. When he went back to Chicago, Louis and Zutty were working together in a band led by Carroll Dickerson at the Savoy Ballroom. Earl was so annoyed for a while that he avoided his former friends. He took a job with clarinetist Jimmie Noone's band at the Apex Club.

One night Earl played George Gershwin's "Rhapsody in Blue," an American composition in the European tradition but influenced by the feeling of American jazz. Afterward, Earl went to the men's room, where a young white man told Earl he played the Gershwin composition very well. Earl thanked him. Then the men's room attendant told Earl that the white man was Gershwin himself.

Hines left the Apex Club to lead a band at the Grand Terrace Ballroom, a new club at Oakwood and South Parkway, in December 1928. The club was designed to be a glamorous, fashionable place featuring the best entertainers. A nationally renowned tap dancer, Bill "Bojangles" Robinson, appeared there. Other performers were famous primarily in the African-American entertainment world—the comedy team of Buck and Bubbles, comedian Billy Mitchell, and singer/dancer Mae Alix, who sang a hit song, "The Butter and Egg Man," about the appeal of a man who had money. After about two years, gangsters muscled their way into the club. It stayed open, but it had to operate under the protection of a very powerful and dangerous mobster, Al Capone.

One night, Hines was sitting in the kitchen while gangsters were meeting in another part of the club. One ran through the kitchen, yelling "The heat's on!" and threw a package containing twelve thousand dollars in Hines's lap. Hines hid the money and had it ready when the gangsters asked him for it a week later. They gave him five hundred dollars for his trouble.[12]

As the club's master of ceremonies, Hines became a well-known bandleader of the swing era. He began broadcasting on a small radio station. Then NBC put him on their lines that went coast to coast and to Canada. When Hines took the band on the road, he found fans everywhere.

During the twelve years until 1940 that Earl Hines and his band worked at the Grand Terrace, nearly every great name in the African-American entertainment world had an engagement with him. Talented young pianists around the country dreamed of careers in music when they heard Hines's broadcasts. Jay McShann heard them in Oklahoma. His mother used to call out to him, "What are you doing up so late?" "My homework," he used to say. But he was listening to Hines.[13] Nat Cole, then a teenage pianist, later to be a world famous singer, used to stand outside the club and listen to Hines play. Nat would reminisce one day, "Our house was near the old Grand Terrace, and I spent many a night in the alley listening to Earl Hines for ideas."[14]

Hines went on to tour with his band after the Grand Terrace closed in 1940 and again found enthusiastic audiences everywhere he played. His band offered young musicians an opportunity to play for a masterful musician and get exposure.

But it had been in the 1920s, when he recorded with Armstrong, that Hines created his innovative style of playing jazz piano. Precisely what he did was use his right hand to play in the upper register of the piano, an octave above the usual melody line, to emulate the clarion call of the trumpet. The style, achieved by playing in octaves, as musicians say — playing the exact same notes an octave apart — allowed him to place the melody and harmonic background of a song in bold relief. His right hand could be heard clearly in a big group. He claimed that he developed this "trumpet style" [15] of playing when he worked with the Lois Deppe band and became fascinated by trumpeter Joe Smith.

Striders to Beboppers and Beyond

With Armstrong, Hines also started playing a tremolo of two notes with his right hand. The notes sounded like a trumpeter's vibrato. Perhaps Smith was Hines's first role model. But if anyone could inspire a pianist to yearn for a clarion call like the trumpet's and a warm, emotional vibrato, it was Armstrong.

Projecting the sound of the piano with his trumpet style, Hines was able to play long, melodic lines effectively; explore sophisticated harmonic ideas, especially with inverted chords—chords that included all the notes of written chords but were voiced in a different order, not necessarily the way they had been written; left hand melodies; and a subtle, rhythmic feeling with abrupt changes of tempo and rhythm. All the while, his playing was buoyant with his assertiveness and charm. Hines was a great innovator, who found new ways to make music more interesting.

One early pianist deeply affected by Hines was Milt Buckner, a swinging pianist-arranger, who used a "locked hands" style, playing "block chords."[16] That means he played in octaves with his right hand and adapted a stride style with his left hand, to make sure he could be heard in Lionel Hampton's band in the 1940s.

When a romantic-sounding baritone, Billy Eckstine, joined the Hines band in the early 1940s and, on the spur of the moment for a recording date, composed lyrics and sang them for a blues tune, "Jelly, Jelly," the Hines band reached the height of its popularity. Billy also sang the band's other major hit, "Stormy Monday Blues."

Hines had an important turnover of personnel in 1942. His tenor saxophonist Budd Johnson quit. Earl hired alto saxophonist Charlie Parker, and trumpeter Dizzy Gillespie joined, too. Gillespie and Parker were starting a revolution of their own. Parker switched to play tenor for Earl's band, but he played it the same way he played his alto—with increasingly adventuresome harmonies and rhythms at very fast tempos. That was the way Dizzy played trumpet. Eventually they would make the music of the swing era sound old-fashioned.

40

The Dominant Pianists of the Swing Era

The youngsters left Hines's band at the end of 1942 and began concentrating on their own style. They wrote intense compositions with new, strange-sounding harmonies based on the chord structures of old songs. Drummers for their groups invented clipped, abrupt polyrhythms. Journalists called the new style of music "bebop," because the word sounded like the choppy drum rhythms. The name caught on.

When the beboppers began recording in the early 1940s, musicians all around the country heard the records. Youngsters started playing the new music with its advanced harmonies. The music seemed to reflect the intense emotions generated by World War II for all Americans, and the intense fight by African-Americans fed up with racial prejudice in the country.

At the time the beboppers left Hines, they were still struggling. It would be another few years before big bands became less popular and Parker and Gillespie could make their influence felt. The hip, bebop style didn't usurp the popularity of swing. But at the same time, the draft for World War II stripped the bands of musicians. When they came home, many bands didn't exist anymore. Small groups had become popular instead, founded by musicians who hadn't gone to war.

The small group sound had its roots in swing, and the pianists used the innovations of Earl Hines. Nat "King" Cole, who became a millionaire and an international star in the 1940s and 1950s as a pianist and singer with his King Cole Trio, always said that Hines was the master. From Hines, Cole had learned to play with swing and harmonic sophistication. Though not a bebopper, Cole also played with intimations of the complex new harmonies. The public loved that dash of intensity.

Most of all, economics brought about the end of the big band era. Leaders found it too expensive to keep their bands traveling. In 1948, many of them, including Earl Hines's, folded all at once. Hines's heyday as a bandleader ended, while young musicians were busy extending the ideas of Hines's generation.

Duke Ellington's band was
"beyond category,"
as he liked to say about
great performers.

Duke Ellington and Count Basie

Duke Ellington, beginning in the 1920s, and Count Basie, starting in the 1930s, used the piano to orient their great creations, which were their bands and the music they played. It sometimes seemed to casual listeners that these pianists made their personal styles subordinate to the good of the bands. Actually, though, the pianists set the tone for their bands — Duke with his compositions for his jazz concert orchestra, and Basie with his arrangements for his brassy, blues-based band. The other instrumentalists played the music that these pianists conceived of for the whole group, and then the pianists played accompaniment for their groups. It was as if these bandleaders actually accompanied themselves.

No band ever sounded like Duke's. To compose, Duke used the strengths of his musicians as his inspiration and guide. With his roots in stride, particularly the style of James P. Johnson, he developed as a percussive player as well as an harmonic explorer, hitting odd, dissonant notes and chords to inspire and signal his musicians. He told them when to come in and what to play, and they created exquisite, adventurous music. Sometimes he simply talked his new arrangements to his men instead of writing the music for them. The band, rather than the piano alone, served as his instrument.

Basie had also begun as a protégé of the stride stylists, particularly Fats Waller with his powerful, rocking left hand. Eventually Basie pared down his piano style to a minimum. With a few notes struck rather lightly, he could set his bold band on an exultantly swinging course. His band musicians became his left hand and also embellished and improvised as much on his right hand as they did on the arrangements they played.

Ellington became one of the most talked-about musicians in the world, after he took his band into the Cotton Club in Harlem in 1927. He began playing his own music there. Now he is regarded as one of the greatest composers of American music. Jazz musicians call it American Classical Music.

Striders to Beboppers and Beyond

Basie's launching pad was the Club Reno, when the Pendergast machine ruled Kansas City. Broadcast on shortwave radio from the Reno, the Basie band's music reached the ears of clarinetist Benny Goodman in Chicago. Goodman described the experience to John Hammond, an important New York City-based record producer and talent scout for jazz and blues players. Hammond and an agent rushed to Kansas City to sign Basie to recording and performing contracts.

With Jimmy Rushing as the band vocalist singing the blues, Basie's band toured in the South and made its way to New York. The band smoothed out its rough spots, enjoyed a popular engagement on 52nd Street, and traveled the world, as Duke's band did.

After both leaders died—Duke in 1974, and Basie in 1984—the bands kept working under new leaders. Ellington's son Mercer inherited and led the band for twenty-one years until his death. Former Basie band members followed Basie. Of course, neither band ever sounded quite the same as when their creators had conducted from their pianos with their unique styles. But their classic bands recorded so much music during the lifetimes of the leaders that the bins in music stores overflow with compact discs of all types, from the beginning to the end of each leader's career.

Many times both pianists said they were influenced by the stride pianists—and Earl Hines.

Jay McShann

Hines—and Tatum, too—also influenced talented and musically curious blues pianists. With Kansas City as home base, Jay McShann formed a band and toured the country, until he was drafted in 1944. Finding the music world changed after he spent thirteen months in the Army, he worked with a small group in the late 1940s. The group played at the Suzie Q club in Los Angeles with a prominent blues singer, Jimmy Witherspoon. And McShann became friends with and an ardent admirer of Art Tatum.

McShann decided to attend the University of Kansas City's Conservatory of Music to develop a formal understanding of the music he had been playing through the years. "I never did read any piano music," he explained, "so I went to school in 1951 and '52 to get an overall view of music."[17] He developed from a traditional blues player into a modern one. When asked to describe his style, he said that he played like himself: "The left hand carries the right hand, which tells the story." He developed such polish and clarity that when he starred in a Kool Jazz Festival concert in New York in the mid-1980s, he stole the show with his feeling, vitality and polished technique. In the 1990s, he could still pack the venerated Village Vanguard jazz club.

Teddy Wilson

Teddy Wilson learned about the new swing music by listening to Earl "Fatha" Hines's recordings with Louis Armstrong. Eventually adding his own ideas—his voicings of the chords and his substitutions and improvisations—Wilson became one of the most important and influential pianists in the 1930s. He played long, melodic lines, and his sense of swing was quietly executed. Outstanding about his style were his clarity and tasteful, light touch. So refined and smooth was his sound that he sometimes was accused of having little in common with mainstream African-American jazz. But his fans recognized his sparkiness and loved the brilliance of his performances as a leader, arranger, and accompanist.

Born on November 24, 1912 in Austin, Texas, he moved with his mother, father, and at least one elder brother, Gus, to Tuskegee, Alabama in 1918. Other African-Americans were leaving the South, but Teddy's father became head of the English Department at Tuskegee Institute and Teddy's mother the chief librarian. In school, Teddy played several instruments, including the piano, without enthusiasm. Gradually he fell in love with instrumental jazz by listening to recordings of cornetist Bix

Striders to Beboppers and Beyond

Beiderbecke, trombonist Frankie Trumbauer, and trumpeter Joe "King" Oliver, Armstrong's mentor.

At age sixteen, Wilson visited Chicago and heard big city, professional jazz players—McKinney's Cotton Pickers, the swinging bands of the brothers Fletcher and Horace Henderson, and some of the great saxophonists and trumpeters in those groups. They inspired Teddy. His mother implored him to go to college, and so he spent a year at Talladega in Alabama. But he couldn't resist the allure of jazz, and he headed for Detroit's jazz scene.

In Detroit, Teddy began playing with "territory bands" (regional groups), in which trumpeter Roy Eldridge and trombonist Vic Dickenson—both destined to become important jazz players in the swing era—were getting their start. Even more important for Teddy, he moved to Toledo, Ohio, in 1931, where he heard Art Tatum playing on a radio show and in clubs. Teddy became profoundly affected by Tatum's mastery of harmonies and bravura runs. Tatum's gift for improvising harmonies was so great that when other instrumentalists played with him, they held him back. It's possible that Wilson's talent and refined sensibilities impressed Tatum. Teddy was playing tenths with his left hand and long, flowing, improvised lines with his right. The pianists became friends and went out together at night, jamming on little upright pianos in Toledo's after-hours clubs.

By 1931, Wilson moved to Chicago, where he heard Earl Hines at the Grand Terrace. Wilson thought Tatum had the greatest command of the piano, but Hines's authority as a jazz player mesmerized Wilson. Teddy told Stanley Dance in the 1970s, "Strictly in terms of the jazz idiom, Earl Hines has . . . the most powerful rhythmic drive, more so than Art or even Fats. . . . Earl had this original concept of playing the piano rather like a horn, with an eccentric bass against it implying the rhythm. . . . Earl would be playing between the beats with his left hand, which pianists are doing today."[18] Everything Hines did instructed Wilson.

Wilson had the chance to play with several important Chicago bands, including Louis Armstrong's and Jimmie Noone's. When Hines took his

46

band on a tour, Teddy worked at the Grand Terrace with a substitute band. In New York City, John Hammond, a very important talent scout for Columbia Records, heard Teddy on a broadcast and sent for him. In New York, Wilson worked in groups under the leadership of alto saxophonist, trumpeter, composer, and arranger Benny Carter, and moved to another group, establishing a reputation for his freshness and artistry in New York. Carter had taught Teddy to learn songs from sheet music before he made changes or substitutions. After all, sometimes the exact note written by the composer was the best one.

He moved to Harlem with his wife, Irene, a pianist and songwriter, whom he had met in Chicago. (In one of those odd twists of fate, Earl Hines had watched from a club one night when her previous husband had picked a fight with a notorious tough guy on the South Side. The two men had shot and killed each other in the street.) Like Teddy, Irene inspired audiences with her playing. However, like most women musicians at that time, she had little opportunity to advance her career. Jazz musicians rarely hired women players.

Then Teddy fell in love with a neighbor in their apartment building. The breakup of her marriage led Irene to write a poignant song, "Some Other Spring," which became a jazz standard. She remarried eventually and wrote many fine songs under the name Irene Wilson Kitchings. Billie Holiday recorded her song, "I'm Pulling Through." Teddy remarried, too, several times.

John Hammond doted upon Teddy Wilson and introduced him to other musicians. Wilson played for a jam session with clarinetist Benny Goodman and drummer Gene Krupa at singer Mildred Bailey's house in 1935. After that, the three musicians recorded for Victor. Hammond also arranged for a recording series with Teddy Wilson, first under his own name, featuring singer Billie Holiday. A few years later, Teddy played for Billie's group for the Brunswick label, which was sold to Columbia. The recordings were that company's "race records."

The Wilson-Holiday recordings were done with many of the great African-American and white sidemen and soloists of the swing era, among them Count Basie's band members. Eventually the recordings became recognized as jazz classics. They continue to be reissued and played continually all around the world. Of the many times Billie record-ed such tunes as "What a Little Moonlight Can Do," her 1935 version done with Wilson remains one of her best. She was singing with a clear voice and unmannered style in those days, and she had his exquisitely tasteful accompaniment.

On Easter Sunday in 1936, Teddy played a concert led by Benny Goodman with Gene Krupa in a Chicago club. Theirs was regarded as the first interracial group to perform in America. A few months later, vibes player Lionel Hampton, also African-American, joined the group. The delicacy and swing of the pianist, vibraphonist, and clarinetist, and the fieriness and showmanship of the drummer, made musical history. On January 16, 1938, Goodman took a big band, whose fame had been spreading, into Carnegie Hall. Included in the concert, which established Goodman and Krupa as major stars, was the trio with Teddy. The con-cert turned out to be a milestone in jazz. The trio plus Hampton per-formed together in the years to come and has been immortalized on recordings, film, and videos.

Teddy Wilson recalled how Hammond had encouraged Goodman to form the trio and Goodman had done it against the advice of his man-agers: "They told Goodman he was a promising young clarinetist and he'd ruin his career by bringing me in. The public proved just the oppo-site. His band was just about international anyway. There were Jewish players, Irish, Italian, southerners, it didn't matter. Goodman picked men on the basis of their music. That was his whole life. . . . Anyway, the enthusiasm was tremendous. The Benny Goodman Trio was almost like the Beatles became later. People were hysterical. They went wild."[19]

Goodman's venture helped integrate jazz. Musicians had been learn-ing from each other and often admiring each other's work enormously throughout the history of the music, with African-Americans as the inno-vators and whites as the pioneering promoters. Whites helped popular-ize the music with white audiences.

Teddy Wilson, one of the most influential stylists beginning in the swing era, was renowned for his elegance and touch at the keyboard.
Here he is at the piano with the Benny Goodman band in 1953 (Benny is third from left).

Wilson worked in CBS studios throughout the 1940s and 1950s, appeared in a musical revue, *The Seven Lively Arts*, with Benny Goodman, and played in the movie *The Benny Goodman Story* in 1956. He also taught piano at Juilliard in the 1940s and 1950s. Without ever corrupting the purity and clarity of his style, he held audiences rapt for the rest of his life. The polish, the rhythmic momentum, and the brightness of his melodic improvisations earned him enduring respect.

In 1974, Wilson toured in South America with Marian McPartland, who had taken some of her earliest lessons from his recordings, Ellis Larkins, who had studied piano at Juilliard, and Earl Hines, who had been the "Fatha" to all of them. In the 1970s and early 1980s, Teddy performed with one of his sons, a bassist, in such clubs as Bradley's, the foremost jazz piano-bass duo room in New York. Teddy died of cancer in 1986.

Shortly before his death, Teddy was a guest on "Piano Jazz," a prize-winning radio show hosted by Marian McPartland. His fingers were as easeful and light on the keys as dancer Fred Astaire's feet had been on the ground. Marian told Teddy jokingly that she wondered if a pianist could be so relaxed he might slip off the piano bench. He said, "You have to have some tension to sound the note." But there was never a second of stress in his sound.[20]

Mary Lou Williams

Men players liked to say that women couldn't play jazz as well as men. But they certainly never said that about Mary Lou Williams. Born Mary Alfrieda Scruggs on May 8, 1910 in Atlanta, Georgia, she began playing the piano by ear when she was three. Her family moved to East Liberty, near Pittsburgh, Pennsylvania. A child prodigy, Mary Lou at age six was hired to play at parties, some for wealthy white families such as the Mellons in Pittsburgh. Her stepfather gave her pocket money to play his favorite tunes and took her to local clubs and theaters, where she became known as "the piano girl."[21] She was so impressive that professional musicians passing through town went to her house to hear her, and they were thrilled.

In junior high school, she received some formal education from a music teacher. Her poor family was growing large. She would eventually have ten half brothers and sisters. So at age fourteen, to earn money for the family, she took a job as a pianist with a touring vaudeville show. She loved to be around musicians anyway. "I had that blood in me like a gypsy," she later said. "I wanted to go out and play, be with musicians."[22] It wasn't all fun, though; for example, she had to fight off the advances of the man running the show. She called life on the road an "animal life."[23]

At age fifteen, working full-time in a small band, she met baritone saxophonist John Williams, who helped protect her on the road. Two years later, she married him. They toured to work, recording in Chicago in a group led by John and playing in Kansas City and Oklahoma City. Then they joined Andy Kirk's Twelve Clouds of Joy, a band that was touring the Southwest. Mary Lou was taken along because she could arrange and compose. She also drove a car for the band. Finally, she broke through the barrier of prejudice against woman players.

She recalled, "I'd wait outside ballrooms in the car, and if things were bad and people weren't dancing, they would send somebody to get me and I'd go in and play 'Froggy Bottom' [her own song] or some other boogie-woogie number—and things would jump. It may have been that they didn't want a woman in the band because women during that era were not really allowed to be in with a group of men. That made people scream and carry on, because they saw a woman that weighed about ninety pounds—to hear me play so heavy, like a man, that was something else."[24]

In 1928, the band settled into Kansas City's jumping scene. Mary Lou found herself in demand as musicians discovered her abilities. They would tap on her window in the middle of the night to call her for jam sessions. By 1931, she was first pianist for Kirk's band, and Kirk helped her with chords and voicings so she could write down her arrangements. By the time she was twenty-five, she was acknowledged to be the arranging force behind Kirk's band. Other famous bandleaders, white and African-American, including Armstrong, Hines, Ellington, Goodman, Tommy Dorsey, and Jimmie Lunceford, asked her to write for them.

In 1936, she did a new arrangement of "Froggy Bottom," which made the Kirk band hot with the public. She wrote for many bands by flashlight as she traveled by night in the car that carried the Kirk band hundreds of miles between engagements. She was earning three to fifteen dollars per arrangement. But she didn't keep good track of copyrights for the arrangements and the royalties due her. By the time she left the Kirk band in 1942, she had recorded over one hundred sides with it. She tried and failed to win legal rights to some of her songs and arrangements.

Exactly why she left Kirk's band isn't clear. She may have become tired of writing in a certain style for Kirk. She didn't have the chance to experiment. Her struggle for legal rights to royalties may have caused tension. She also divorced John Williams and went home to Pittsburgh, where she led a little band. Then she fell in love with a trumpeter, Shorty Baker. Together they joined Duke Ellington's band in 1943. In less than a year, Mary Lou left the band and Baker and moved to Harlem.

Her apartment became a favorite gathering place for gifted young beboppers to meet, play, experiment, and discuss music. She gave lessons to Thelonious Monk, a young pianist involved in bebop's development who had already been mightily influenced by James P. Johnson. Pianist Bud Powell, a star among the young beboppers, visited Mary Lou, too. All of them inspired each other. Monk and Bud were the most innovative pianists of the bebop movement.

Mary Lou played for the Café Society clubs, one in Greenwich Village and one on the Upper East Side. Their owner, Barney Josephson, liked Mary Lou's music so much that he helped her get her own radio show on WNEW on Sundays in 1945. Between 1943 and 1945, she kept growing technically and artistically as an arranger and composer.

She wrote the music for "The Zodiac Suite," naming the parts of it for signs of the zodiac and dedicating each part to her musician friends. Through Josephson's contacts, her suite found its way to a performance with an orchestra at Town Hall in New York. An arranger, Milt Orent, who was then working for NBC, assisted her in writing down the arrangements. The critics in 1946 appreciated her music; her mastery of harmony was particularly evident. And the "Gemini" section of the suite bore a remarkable resemblance in its harmonies to some of Duke Ellington's music.

For the next six years, Mary Lou worked in New York, deeply influenced by Dizzy Gillespie and the other revolutionary beboppers. She worried very little about her failed marriages. "I just can't keep husbands or sweethearts," she was reported to have said in 1944, and the comment was used for the liner notes for "The Zodiac Suite" on a compact disc released on Vintage Jazz Classics. "I forget about them. I forget about friends, too. I guess the only thing I really love is music."[25]

People who knew her well agreed with this analysis. In 1952, Mary Lou, then forty-three, went to play in London and Germany. By 1953, she landed in Paris, where a twenty-nine-year-old drummer, Gerard Pochenet, was called to play a record date with her, along with bassist Buddy Banks and saxophonist Don Byas. "Don Byas had been sweet on her years before in Kansas City, and so he played his best on that day in Paris," Gerard recalled.[26]

Gerard thought she was an attractive woman, though she dressed in plain clothes and wore her hair in a simple pageboy. Only on stage did she wear a silk dress. After their recording date, Gerard, Mary Lou, and Don Byas went for dinner. "I had no idea of romance at that dinner. Mary Lou looked and acted like a woman, of course, but she was forthright, outspoken, not particularly feminine." (Another American woman pianist, Hazel Scott, was more ebullient. She went to live in Paris, where she held fancy parties and became friends with important people in government and the arts. Hazel taught French people to say "Je te dig" —

"I dig you.") "We talked about music. It was the main link. Music came first with Mary Lou. And she was so gifted, not only because she worked at it, but also by instinct."

During the next three months, Mary Lou and Gerard began a love affair. By April, 1954, six months after they had met, she moved into Gerard's family chateau a short train trip away from Paris. Mary Lou and Gerard's grandmother got along very well, though neither spoke a word of the other's language.

Mary Lou never learned French. "Mary Lou was not interested in things French. The people we saw were Americans who spoke English. . . . And the music was exciting. She was not interested in seeking out anything more than the music. She never went to the opera once. We went to clubs to hear other jazz musicians. . . . She listened only to jazz. She was particularly impressed by Art Tatum and Erroll Garner — but who isn't? . . . She was neither a dresser nor a gourmet, not interested in the clothes or food in Paris. She would eat because she was hungry but felt nothing special for food. She was simply a great influence on other musicians. She had the knack to be a musician's musician. . . . I thought I wanted to marry her. I couldn't care less about race. In France it was not a problem. . . . Mary Lou was a fount of information. That fascinated me. Music was the common bond."[27]

In December 1954, she went back to the United States. Gerard hoped she would return to Paris. But by spring 1955, he was receiving letters from her about her growing preoccupation with religion. She and Gerard would never pick up the strings of their relationship.

Mary Lou's friend, Thelma Carpenter, who had sung with bands led by Teddy Wilson and Count Basie, thought Mary Lou fell in love with sounds. "She was a loner except in music. If you didn't talk about music, she had no conversation for you. Later in her life, some of Mary Lou's family became important to her. But if the music was right, all was fine. She once told an interviewer on television, 'You can't interview me. I can't talk. I only play. You can tell a story on the keyboard.' "[28] Gerard also knew that Mary Lou had loved her mother and relatives, but he thought she had come from "a confusing family structure, maybe a confusing childhood altogether," he said.[29]

Mary Lou became depressed by the way drugs and alcohol ravaged some musicians who were her close friends. She virtually retired from performing for a few years, and she converted to Roman Catholicism. In 1957, Dizzy Gillespie convinced her to play with his modern jazz orchestra. She became involved in music again as the head of a foundation intended to reach out, through music and education, to the poor and the hopeless. She received Guggenheim fellowships, National Endowment for the Arts grants, and honorary degrees from eight colleges. She became an artist-in-residence at Duke University in North Carolina, where she taught jazz and music appreciation.

In the late 1970s, Sumi Tonooka, who was studying jazz piano and composition in a Philadelphia college, found Mary Lou's New York phone number in a musician's union book. Sumi called and asked for lessons. Mary Lou invited Sumi to her apartment. Sumi was overwhelmed by the honor of playing Mary Lou's piano. Thelonious Monk, Bud Powell, and many other famous pianists had played it. Monk especially had caused Sumi to fall in love with jazz when Sumi's father took her to a club on her birthday to hear Monk. Sumi learned most of all simply by watching Mary Lou play. As Sumi described it, "She had so much history in her playing."[30]

Mary Lou had grown through ragtime, boogie-woogie, the blues, swing, and bebop. She died on May 29, 1981, leaving her estate to the Mary Lou Williams Foundation to pay for gifted children to study with professional musicians.

CHAPTER THREE
Disciples of the Early Jazz Piano Masters

Hines, Tatum, Wilson, Basie, Duke, and Mary Lou—these were among the most influential jazz pianists, not only in the United States but in Europe and Japan. Nat "King" Cole idolized Earl Hines, and in turn, Nat Cole's swinging piano-bass-guitar trio of the 1940s influenced many pianists.

Among them was Ahmad Jamal, who in the 1950s took inspiration from Cole and became a great commercial success. Jamal moved from his native Pittsburgh to Chicago, where he struggled to earn a living with musical and nonmusical jobs. Eventually he formed a trio like Nat Cole's. But Jamal tried a drummer instead of a guitarist, for a harder, more aggressive sound. His trio's recording of the song "Poinciana" vaulted him to stardom.

Trumpeter Miles Davis, who had played with Charlie Parker and Dizzy Gillespie, began leading his own groups. He paid special attention to Ahmad Jamal's pacing. Jamal gave his sidemen a great deal of room to play solos. The silences, or spaces, between piano solos enhanced the drama of the entire performance. Miles Davis's very influential groups of the 1950s and 1960s—and all of them for the rest of his life, actually—owed a debt to the pioneering jazz pianists.

Milt Buckner's "locked hands" style in Lionel Hampton's band influenced a blind pianist, George Shearing, in England. He was learning by ear from American jazz musicians in live performances and on recordings. It took Shearing several decades of struggle, but he finally moved to the United States and established himself as a brilliant jazz pianist and group leader with the George Shearing Quintet in the 1950s.

In his group, Shearing played swinging American standards and Latin music with a "locked hands" style. He explained that this meant playing "a four note chord in the right hand with the left hand doubling the little finger melody played in the right hand, the whole structure occurring within one octave."[1] The vibes in his group repeated Shearing's melody above his line, and the guitar did the same an octave below the piano's lines. It wasn't an orchestral approach to the piano, but when the public heard the quintet's version of "September in the Rain," a starring group was born.

Shearing became quite famous. The owners of Birdland, a world-famous club regarded as the hub of jazz, asked him to write its theme song. Sitting at his dinner table, he composed "Lullaby of Birdland" in his head. It became one of the best known of all jazz songs.

British-born Marian McPartland, too, kept listening to recordings by American jazz musicians, particularly the pianists, when she was a child. Among her favorites were Teddy Wilson, Mary Lou Williams, and a more obscure jazz and boogie-woogie pianist named Cleo Patra Brown.

Marian's parents disapproved of her concentrating on the piano and thought it was eccentric when she insisted on studying classical music at the Guild Hall School. Then Marian upset her parents so much when she went on a tour with a popular music group that she changed her last name for professional purposes. (Her maiden name was Turner; she

57

changed it to Page.) During World War II, entertaining American soldiers in Europe, she met an American cornetist, Jimmy McPartland, from the Austin High Gang in Chicago. They married in Germany, and in the 1940s, she went to the United States as "Jimmy's war bride," as she put it.[2]

Her career, like Mary Lou's, spanned all the eras and changing styles of jazz. Marian became one of the few truly successful women jazz instrumentalists—all but one of them pianists. (That one exception was trombonist Melba Liston.) In the male-dominated jazz world, women were accepted only as pianists until the 1980s.

In Tokyo, Japan, after World War II, American jazz recordings were so expensive that ordinary people couldn't afford them. But coffee shop owners bought them from American military men and installed expensive sound systems to attract customers. A young woman pianist, Toshiko Akiyoshi, born in Manchuria, China, who was studying in Tokyo, went to a jazz coffee shop. There she heard Teddy Wilson's records. She fell in love with them and kept going back "to learn new material," she recalled.[3]

Toshiko learned to play jazz by ear. Then she fell under the spell of bebop pianist Bud Powell. American jazz musicians visiting Japan, hearing how gifted she was, encouraged her to move to the United States. She decided to study jazz at the Berklee School of Music in Boston, cofounded a prize-winning big band with her husband, saxophonist Lew Tabackin, and became a highly regarded composer and arranger.

Born in Algiers, Algeria, in North Africa, Martial Solal moved to Paris in the 1940s to write scores for movies, play with excellent French and American musicians, and find himself acknowledged for his vibrant style as an international star. In Argentina, Lalo Schifrin was discovered by Dizzy Gillespie on tour in South America. Gillespie brought Schifrin to the United States in the 1960s, where Schifrin distinguished himself as a composer and arranger for movies.

Disciples of the Early Jazz Piano Masters

In the Soviet Union and other Communist-controlled countries, jazz was banned. Jazz musicians risked persecution and arrest for listening to jazz on "The Voice of America" radio broadcasts. Nevertheless, the musicians listened, shared their scarce records, learned to play by ear, and flocked to jazz concerts when their governments began allowing American jazz musicians to visit on tours.

These are a representative handful of players from around the world who heard jazz on the radio and records and fell in love with the liberating style. In Europe and Japan especially, young players committed themselves to playing jazz, and American musicians have been treated with great respect abroad, even in times when they felt their music was not fully appreciated in the United States.

CHAPTER FOUR
The BeBop Pianists

Young Dizzy Gillespie and Charlie "Bird" Parker, who worked on adventurous new harmonies in Earl Hines's band, used to go to Minton's Playhouse in Harlem in the early 1940s to experiment. They were joined there by very important pianists, especially the great creative genius, Thelonious Monk. He played in the house trio at Minton's. Essentially a self-taught musician, he knew more about harmonies than all of the other young revolutionaries put together.

The young revolutionaries approached popular songs in a radically new way. Instead of playing them in a straightforward manner, they took the chord structures of the tunes, changed them in many ways, and created new chords, melodies, and songs. They also changed the rhythms and phrasing of songs. The new and altered music acquired fresh names. "How High the Moon," for example, became a tune called "Ornithology."

The chords (which jazz musicians called changes) to Gershwin's "I Got Rhythm" inspired bebop musicians to write thousands of songs. Tadd Dameron, a piano-playing composer and arranger, wrote a tune called "Hot House" based on the chords of "What Is This Thing Called Love?"

The beboppers put flatted fifths in their songs. The pop song writers hadn't done that. A flatted fifth means that the fifth note in any scale is played a half step down from the usual whole step in the scale. The bebop revolutionaries fell in love with flatted fifths, and they began putting them in everything they played or wrote.

The rhythms in bebop had to be compatible with the new music. A young drummer of the time, Kenny Clarke, kept time not on the bass drum but on the cymbals; he used the bass drum for accents. Clarke's technique became known as "dropping bombs." Clarke also began playing many rhythms in one song—polyrhythms—to a greater degree than older drummers had done. Clarke broke up the rhythm, making it more diversified. And the bebop musicians often played their intense music at breakneck speed. Bassists embellished and complicated their harmonies and time-keeping chores, too, and played their own improvised solos.

Some very fine musicians from the swing era couldn't and didn't want to play bebop. It sounded strange and dissonant. In the long run, most of the older players accepted the new music and incorporated its adventures with melodies, harmonies, and rhythms into their work.

Thelonious Monk had been experimenting with chords by himself for a long time and was fascinated with dissonance. At Minton's, he showed Dizzy various chords on the piano. Dizzy used all the notes in Monk's D-minor chord as the melody line of one of his most famous compositions, "A Night in Tunisia." And Dizzy added a Latin rhythm. Dizzy, Monk, and Kenny Clarke spent hours together experimenting with bebop in the early 1940s. Other musicians came to hear their exciting new music, too.

Soon a young drummer named Max Roach and an odd young pianist, Bud Powell, became part of the bebop clique. At first, beboppers—except for the house band—could only jam for free at Minton's.

Striders to Beboppers and Beyond

By the mid-1940s, though, they were able to find paid bookings in the hip clubs on West 52nd Street. Bebop spread and inspired more musicians to explore and diversify the sound of jazz.

Hundreds of pianists—and singers, bandleaders, and all the other instrumentalists, too—were affected by bebop. The pianists in groups led by Dizzy and Bird or by Dizzy alone were Monk, Bud, George Wallington (a white protégé of Bud's who did whatever Dizzy needed), John Lewis, who was fresh out of the army, Billy Taylor, an African-American college graduate, and Al Haig and Joe Albany, two white pianists. The racial makeup of his groups wasn't important to Dizzy. He wanted musicians who understood what he was doing. To him the most important thing a pianist could do for a bebop group was to play accompaniment and stay out of the way of the horn players—and show up on time for performances.

Among the pianists, Monk became recognized as one of the greatest composers in jazz, and his ideas and sounds continue to challenge and inspire musicians. His music had quirky, angular chords and rhythms; it was haunting, rich, and difficult music to play, and his contribution through his compositions was most of all harmonic and spiritual. His best-known song, "Round Midnight," is a voyage into a mysterious, moody time of day when people sometimes reflect upon their lives. No other composer of American songs captured that extreme mood so well.

Bud Powell, a fiery soloist, set a standard for the performances of bebop stylists. He affected, to one degree or another, the styles of all the jazz pianists who came after him. His strength was in his right hand, which played long, melodic, very intense, saxophone-like lines. Both pianists, unfortunately, led tortured lives.

Thelonious Monk

Monk, who became known as the High Priest of Bebop, was born on October 10, 1917, in Rocky Mount, North Carolina. At an early age he moved with his close-knit family to San Juan Hill in New York City. His mother, sister, and brother tried to protect him in a world he always seemed to find harsh and complex. By his teen years, he was earning a little money as a musician.

Early in life, too, he met a girl named Nellie, who decided to love, protect, and nurture his talent. They had two children, and for many years they were inseparable. She traveled with him, coddled him, and dealt with all his special needs. *In Straight, No Chaser*, a documentary movie made about him and named for one of his songs, she is shown helping him get through such routine chores as checking into an airport for a flight, while he danced around in circles, lost in his own thoughts about music. He behaved in eccentric ways, because it inspired him to unsettle and surprise other people, and he knew that his attention-getting antics were good publicity for his image as a mystic.

Monk had already learned a great deal about playing from the stride stylists, James P. Johnson and Fats Waller, and he had studied Duke Ellington's style and compositions, before he became the house pianist at Minton's. It was no secret in the jazz world that Monk's instruction to Dizzy about harmonies was invaluable to the young trumpeter and to the bebop revolution. When musicians came to Minton's and couldn't play the new music, Monk was one of the musicians who ran the inadequate players off the stage by playing at very fast tempos and jumping around with key changes.

In those days, Monk communicated fairly well with friends and musicians whom he admired. A trumpeter named Johnny Carisi, for example, went to jam at Minton's; since he was able to keep up with the beboppers, Monk invited him to the bar to have a drink. Carisi said he didn't drink much. Monk told him, "What? Call yourself a jazz player. . . ." Carisi began drinking double gins with Monk.[1]

Dizzy took a group downtown for the first time to play at the Onyx Club on 52nd Street in 1945, and George Wallington went with the group. Dizzy liked Wallington's playing because he stayed out of the way of the horn lines. And when Wallington played a solo, he sounded like his idol, Bud Powell. When Dizzy went to California in 1945 to introduce bebop in a Los Angeles club, he took along pianist Al Haig, another disciple of Bud Powell. Then in 1946, he took a band into the Spotlite, a club on 52nd Street in New York, with Bud Powell on piano. "The money was a little erratic," Dizzy recalled, "and Bud was super-erratic, and I had to do something about that, so I got Monk. I had no trouble outta Monk, not too much, but Monk wasn't showing up on time either. It was against the law to show up on time."[2]

Monk would become infamous for showing up late for appointments. Because Dizzy couldn't stand tardiness, he fired Monk. Kenny Clarke, who was in the band at the Spotlite, brought along his old Army buddy, a young pianist named John Lewis. A very well-educated musician, Lewis had his own arrangements with unusual voicings of chords. It wasn't bebop, and it wasn't swing, but it impressed Dizzy, who took him in. Dizzy's musical director and arranger, Walter Gil Fuller, was terribly upset, because he loved Monk's beautiful, challenging compositions. Dizzy's band played "Tempus Fugit" and many other songs by Bud Powell, and they played "Round Midnight" and other great songs by Monk. But neither of those pianists played in the groups.

The inner circle of beboppers knew how important and original Monk's style and compositions were. The critics didn't agree with them about Monk at first. His flat-fingered style of playing seemed awkward. Critics didn't like his odd compositions, either. And they ridiculed his eccentric personality. Always shy, Monk became even more withdrawn.

A swing era saxophonist went to Monk's house one night and discovered Monk's feelings were hurt because Dizzy and Bird were getting all the credit for bebop. "I'm going to let them take that style and go ahead, and I'm gonna get a new style,"[3] Monk told the horn player. Monk's mother cooked food for the musicians, and Monk played some new, "funny-type" music, the horn player would recall. He loved it. Monk couldn't give it a label. It was simply his music. He wasn't a great piano player, but he fumbled on his piano and created all sorts of dissonant chords. And the horn player heard that Monk's direction and com-

Thelonious Monk (left) was one of the greatest jazz stylists and composers. This photograph of Monk with Howard McGhee, Roy Eldridge, and Teddy Hill was taken in 1948 in front of Minton's Playhouse, where sessions organized by Hill with Monk, Dizzy Gillespie, Charlie "Bird" Parker, and others gave rise to the bebop revolution.

Striders to Beboppers and Beyond

positions were different from Dizzy's. What they had in common was a profound interest in experimenting with harmonies.

There was even some controversy abetted by *Time* magazine about who had invented bebop—Dizzy, Bird, or Monk. "As though all of us and others hadn't played a role," Dizzy said.[4] Monk made his own tortured way in the music world. But his influence on Dizzy was evident. When Dizzy played piano, as he often did, he sounded very much like Monk. Wherever Dizzy traveled, he played Monk's music and made sure audiences knew the composer's name—perhaps to make up for leaving Monk out of bebop's important public victories early on.

Monk worked and lived in obscurity until 1947. Then Blue Note, a record company, gave him a chance to record a variety of songs, including "I Should Care" and Monk's own songs, "I Mean You" and "Round Midnight." The recordings were a commercial failure. His delays and alterations of rhythms, which gave his music a spiky, hesitant sound, and his eerie harmonies, which emphasized the angularity of his style, puzzled the public. Monk felt frustrated and neglected. He had a small, reverential audience in obscure clubs, while his tunes were slowly becoming a staple part of the jazz repertoire.

Orrin Keepnews was an appreciative critic in 1948, when he wrote one of his first jazz articles about Monk for a little magazine called *Record Changer*. Monk was a difficult person to interview. His speech wasn't clear. He tended to give one word answers to questions. But Orrin heard the beauty of Monk's work and called Monk's group an outstanding example of unified small band jazz, with "discipline and coherence," "warmth," "purpose," "coordination," and "a wry, satiric humor that has a rare maturity."[5] Keepnews realized Monk had developed an original piano style, and his band seemed to be shaped to his own manner of playing. Duke Ellington had done the same thing with his band. Keepnews would later be delighted and astonished to find out he had been so correct about Monk.

Monk's next recordings for Blue Note in 1951 weren't financially successful, either. He had the added burden that year of being arrested for heroin possession—though he wasn't using heroin himself. Someone dropped an envelope of heroin at his feet, and the police thought it belonged to Monk. Automatically he lost his cabaret license. That meant he could not perform in New York City clubs. In 1952, he moved to another jazz record label, Prestige, where he found little support. He could make the song "Smoke Gets in Your Eyes," by a musical theater composer, sound as if he had written it himself, so strong and distinctive was his quixotic style. But the public wasn't ready to love it yet.

In 1954, a jazz critic, Nat Hentoff, telephoned the Riverside jazz record label and announced that Monk might make himself available for recordings. Were the producers interested? Orrin Keepnews had become a producer there. So Monk signed with Riverside in 1955, and he did a great deal of his most creative work on recordings with the label.

Orrin found Monk a difficult, stubborn, brilliant genius. He could cause delays in many ways. Once he told a drummer the wrong date to show up for a recording session. Often he was late himself, or he arrived without having rehearsed his music. Orrin told him not to show up for a recording session at all if he was going to come late. For the next session, Monk showed up early. Orrin was late. Monk smiled and said, "What kept you?"[6]

During his first three-year contract with Riverside, Monk's cabaret license was restored. He played with saxophonist John Coltrane at the Five Spot jazz club in Greenwich Village. That group was so successful that Monk was thrust into the spotlight. The public finally accepted him as a great composer and stylist. Even his reputation for moodiness and eccentricity became part of his mystique. When he showed up late for the gigs, people stood in line waiting for hours. He wore unusual hats on the bandstand. He got up from the piano bench and did a little dance. He kept time by shuffling his right foot very noticeably while he played.

He signed again with Riverside in 1958, and the company released an interesting two-disc album of very difficult music called *Brilliance*. It was recorded in two sessions, one in 1956 and the other in 1959. (The first session was released on its own in 1957, winning rave reviews from the critics, and then the two-disc album came out in 1959.) A highlight of the sessions is Monk's song, "Brilliant Corners," which appeared on the first release. He had an all-star cast of musicians—tenor saxophonist Sonny Rollins, drummer Max Roach, bassist Oscar Pettiford, a mainstay of the bebop revolution, trumpeter and fluegelhornist Clark Terry, and alto saxophonist Ernie Henry. For Monk, life really began at age forty.

Columbia, a major label, enticed Monk with money in 1961 and took him away from little Riverside. In 1964, when the Beatles were at the top of the charts, Monk appeared on the cover of *Time* magazine. But success did not improve his mental heath. He suffered through periods of oddness—spells of withdrawal, which doctors never really understood. It didn't help him any that he drank a lot and dabbled in all kinds of drugs. And drugs were all around musicians at that time. The press emphasized his eccentricities. Monk felt ridiculed, his son Thelonious ("T.S.") would recall.[7]

The Newport Jazz Festival hired Monk for the first time in 1958, and he became part of a famous, all-star jazz movie called *Jazz on a Summer's Day*. After that, he toured the world with great success as a pianist and group leader. Usually he met up with appreciative audiences, who adored his music and showmanship. Occasionally, though, he encountered disaster.

Once he and another musician were driving toward Baltimore for a gig with another African-American musician and the Baroness Pannonica de Koenigswater, a wealthy, European-born patroness of jazz musicians, in her very expensive Bentley car. They stopped for a drink at a motel in Delaware. When the police noticed a white woman traveling with two African-Americans, they were pulled over and searched. Nica, as the baroness was called, had a little marijuana in her pocketbook. The police arrested all of them. One of the police hit Monk's hands—"his pianists' hands. I screamed as a crowd gathered," the baroness told Village Vanguard owner Max Gordon for his book, *Live from the Village Vanguard*.[8]

Such indignities did nothing to help the sensitive pianist's state of mind. He was never violent, just odd. Monk's son would always recall that his father was a devoted family man. Despite his depression and his dependence on Nellie, Monk had a positive influence on T.S. The father demonstrated great affection during his lucid periods and good moods. One of his songs, "Little Rootie Tootie," celebrated his son's love affair with a train set.[9] T.S. also thought that his mother, Nellie, an articulate, well-balanced woman, protected the children expertly during Monk's strange moods.

Nellie eventually became exhausted from years of holding the family together and getting Monk to his jobs. They had become very friendly with the baroness, a charming eccentric herself and an heiress in a prominent European banking family, the Rothschilds. The baroness, who was as fascinated by Monk as he was by her wealth and title, began helping Nellie in the 1950s with Monk's care.

Monk kept functioning as a major influence and standard-bearer for other musicians. He taught scores of musicians about how to play his own difficult music and to develop their musicianship. A bassist named Bill Crow remembered a recording session with Monk. Monk tried to teach the musicians the songs by playing them repeatedly. Crow thought that Monk's bass notes were sufficient for the music. Crow didn't think Monk needed a bassist and wasn't sure of what notes to play. The musicians asked Monk to play something easy and familiar for them. He launched into "Tea for Two." That was one of the songs he embellished into a masterpiece, a true art song. But his harmonies were so different from the written song's chords that the musicians, who were supposed to play with him, began laughing hysterically. He told them to keep listening to hear what they should be playing.

Crow began to realize that Monk's intervals—the spaces between the notes in the chords—were ordinary fifths, sixths, and sevenths. It was

Monk's touch and treatment of the notes that made his music sound different from everyone else's. Monk told him, "It can't be any new note. When you look at the keyboard, all the notes are there already. But if you mean a note enough, it will sound different. You got to play the notes you really mean."[10]

Until 1970, Monk worked somewhat consistently in a group that included his loyal tenor saxophonist, Charlie Rouse. But then Monk became increasingly unstable and less interested in working. He still had prestigious bookings, such as tours in Europe in 1971 and 1972 with Dizzy and others in a group called the Giants of Jazz, and a festival in Mexico City, and the Newport Jazz Festivals in New York in the 1970s. Monk was so well respected that he could have worked as much as he wanted to. But he decided to stop playing the piano. Some people thought he lost interest in work because he was depressed. Others thought he had used too many different legal and illegal drugs. Still others thought he had suffered creative burnout—that he had exhausted his body and spirit, and his heart wasn't in his music anymore.

He retreated into Baroness Nica's house in New Jersey. Nica, Monk, and a few other musicians lived on her inheritance. He did not perform again. He left a legacy of more than one hundred original compositions. Among the best known are "Crepuscule with Nellie" and "Pannonica." (The word crepuscule means twilight.) He wrote another song with a woman's name as the title, "Ruby, My Dear," an exceptionally romantic song, in honor of his first love. "Blue Monk," one of his songs for himself, "Rhythm-a-ning," and "Straight, No Chaser" also became very familiar tunes; people recognize many of his songs without knowing the titles. Monk lapsed into a coma and died at age sixty-four in 1982.

Other musicians stayed with Nica while Monk was there. One was pianist Barry Harris. As a young man in Detroit, he had fallen in love with bebop on records. Whenever the beboppers passed through town, he made sure he went to the clubs to hear them. And he discovered he had a talent for teaching music. He used to slow down the records and study every note and nuance. First he taught himself to play bebop, and then he taught other young musicians who loved the new style. In the afternoons, Barry Harris's house became a gathering place for musicians to take lessons. When Barry moved to New York, he remained a teacher as well as a performer. With backing from Nica, he opened a school called the Jazz Cultural Workshop on Eighth Avenue in New York in the 1980s. From all over the world, young musicians arrived to study with Harris, and through him, they received the legacy of the bebop age.

Bud Powell

The other piano titan of the bebop revolution was Bud Powell, whose life was shorter and sadder than Monk's. Powell composed and performed his song, "Tempus Fugit," Latin for "time flies." Occasionally the title is written "Tempus Fugue-It." That version not only suggests that time flies but that Powell had a special affinity for Bach, the European classical composer of fugues. Both ideas are apt. Powell played his song at breakneck speed, with breathtaking technique that graced his beautiful melody, and he learned to love and play classical music as a child.

More than any other song, "Tempus Fugit" shows off how fast, intense and possessed Bud Powell's style could be. A British writer, Max Harrison, described it as a "lucid expression of delirium," which conveyed "the romantic agony of modern jazz."[11] He could also play ballads at less hectic tempos, with such a happy feeling that an ordinary listener would never guess how psychologically troubled Bud was.

Other pianists were in awe of him. They couldn't keep track of all the notes he played. One pianist experienced in transcribing music by ear from recordings believed no one could write down all the notes Bud played. To put his achievement simply, he played very long lines at fast tempos with his right hand, the way Charlie "Bird" Parker played his alto saxophone. At the same time, Bud's left hand played irregularly spaced, dissonant bass notes—bass chords without the stride. His ideas were actually rooted in Earl Hines's horn-like lines and Art Tatum's speed and embellishments. But Bud intensified everything his predecessors had accomplished. He even intensified the intimacy of their sounds.

He electrified audiences with his torrent of music. Nobody ever made Bud sound outdated, and he influenced everyone, even the most virtuosic modernists playing at the end of the twentieth century, to play the way they do. He galvanized all the pianists of his generation and those who came afterward into playing with fierceness and artistry.

To say he had trouble communicating with people when he wasn't playing the piano is a great overstatement. He was mentally ill for all his adult life—and probably to some degree before that. As a teenager, he was shy. He may have always done and said inappropriate things. Saxophonist Dexter Gordon, who played with Bud on West 52nd Street in the early 1940s, said, "Bud was always—ever since I've known him—he was a little on the border line. Because he'd go off into things—expressions, telltale things that would let you know he was off."[12]

Then, in 1945, when he was twenty-one and playing in a band in a Philadelphia club, he was beaten by police. The most probable version of the story is that he got drunk; when the police tried to arrest him for disorderly conduct, they went overboard and beat him around the head. He had never been arrested before. The next day, Bud's band leader called Bud's mother to come and get him. He was too injured to get home by himself.

After the beating, Bud began to have mental breakdowns. Starting in 1947, he went back and forth from recording studios and the jazz world to mental hospitals, where he had electric shock therapy. Pianist Elmo Hope, who had been Bud's friend since their high school days, thought Bud changed a lot after the beating in Philadelphia. Sometimes he had a scowl on his face and a peculiar look in his eyes. Other times, he seemed childlike; he needed help with simple chores, like tying a tie and buttoning a shirt.

On occasion he insulted some of his favorite musicians. He once told the masterful Art Tatum that he had played some wrong notes in a performance. He told Bird that the saxophonist wasn't playing anything of value. Another musician, overhearing Powell, warned him, "Bud, don't talk that way. Bird's your poppa."[13] He meant that Bird was the father of progressive jazz and bebop. Without Bird, Powell's achievements wouldn't exist. Bird himself told people to excuse Bud, because Bird loved the way Bud played.

Some musicians thought Bud was Bird's equal as a player, perhaps even superior. In any case, Bud played the way he did because of Bird's influence. His technique emerged from his studies of classical music and the growing jazz piano tradition, but his style and feeling came from Bird's ideas.

Earl "Bud" Powell was born in New York City into a musical family on September 27, 1924. Family friends said Bud's father was "a fine, old time stride piano player."[14] He claimed that his own father was a great flamenco guitarist who had learned his art when he went to fight in the Spanish American war in Cuba. Both of Bud's brothers played instruments. As a teenager, Bud played for little gigs with his elder brother's band. But Bud did not have a warm relationship with Richie, his very talented younger brother. Richie had to look for encouragement and instruction for his piano playing from friends and musicians outside the family. He became a highly-regarded jazz pianist, but he died young in a car crash in 1956.

Studying the classics as well as the music of James P. Johnson and Fats Waller, Bud devoted himself passionately to music. He was especially inspired by his father. Bebop pianist Walter Davis Jr., who was influenced by Bud, said that Bud's parents and teachers worked him very hard. They wanted him to become a perfect concert artist with European classical music. But Bud preferred to follow Art Tatum and his admirers. One of them, Billy Kyle, took inspiration from both Tatum and Earl Hines; he played in a popular swing era group called the John Kirby sextet and then in Louis Armstrong's group. Bud loved Kyle's work.

During their high school days, Bud and Elmo Hope, another classical music student, spent time together, practicing, playing for each other, and experimenting with jazz. Bud skipped classes to go to the Apollo Theater and worked in groups all around town. After his jobs, he hung

52nd Street in New York in the 1950s; little clubs presenting the greatest jazz musicians in the world thrived here in the 1940s and 1950s.

out in Harlem clubs. Monk, who was seven years older than Bud and working at Minton's, took a liking to Bud. Even though Bud still wasn't playing chords in the bebop style, Monk realized that Bud was talented. Bud was already showing signs of socially unacceptable behavior, too. At Minton's, he put his feet up on a white tablecloth. A waiter wanted to throw him out, but Monk stopped the waiter, saying: "Don't do that. That kid's got talent."[15]

Bud loved Monk's music and began playing it in public in the 1940s, long before the world realized how interesting it was. On Bud's earliest records with the Cootie Williams band in 1944, Bud was still obviously influenced by the runs and flourishes of Tatum's style, but he was beginning to show the effects of Monk's harmonies and Bird's long alto lines and phrasing. In 1945, Bud became part of the clique of young beboppers working on West 52nd Street.

The jazz world was a rough one at that time. Musicians never knew when their jobs would be canceled. Sometimes they played all night and didn't get paid. The perils of their profession made many of them unstable. Their experiences forced them to become very practical. They developed a knack for understanding the ways of the world—an education on the streets. But some of them began drinking far too much as a way of tranquilizing themselves. Some took drugs, too, especially marijuana and heroin.

Jazz historians have observed that Charlie Parker's drug addiction led many young musicians to use heroin. Bird told them not to do it. But youngsters thought they might play more like Bird and make themselves hip and musically brilliant if they imitated his habit. Bud Powell would be remembered by everyone who knew him as a man whose thoughts ran away with him even when he was sober. All it took was one drink, and he became completely unmanageable. He probably wasn't violent, but he looked aggressive and was obviously crazy.

So his genius for playing the piano seems to be all the more miraculous. Perhaps his intensity came from the fire burning out of control in his soul. It was only when he played the piano that he could express himself clearly. Very healthy pianists were unable to organize their music as well as Bud could. In 1949, he made many recordings that were among the best of his, or anyone's, career.

Village Voice critic Gary Giddins wrote an article for a seventieth anniversary celebration of Bud's birth. Giddins speculated that six of Bud's greatest recordings may have been done on the same day in May 1949. They were his own startling composition, "Tempus Fugit," "Celia," named for his daughter, "Cherokee," "I'll Keep Loving You," "Strictly Confidential," and "All God's Chillun' Got Rhythm." Critics thought his recording of "Cherokee" was second only to Bird's.

Bud made all those recordings in 1949 in a time when he was being hospitalized and given electroshock therapy. "Yet here is some of the most mentally and technically stable music in the canon," Gary Giddins wrote. "I have little use for the Van Gogh theory that genius and mental illness are inextricably linked. But the irony can't be ignored."[16] (Van Gogh was one of the greatest European Impressionist painters in the late nineteenth century. Of all the Impressionists, Van Gogh had the worst mental problems. He even cut off one of his own ears as a gesture of love for a woman.) Giddins also asserted that the art of modern jazz piano for the rest of the century stemmed from Powell's performances on the records in 1949, and Bud was one of the century's most important pianists in jazz or any other style of music.

In the early 1950s, Bud married a friend from his childhood. Oscar Goodstein of the Birdland club may have helped the romance get started. Once Bud married Buttercup—that was her nickname—she took over his guardianship and business and financial affairs.

Bud played in one of the decade's most famous jazz concerts, at Massey Hall in Toronto, Canada, in 1953, with Dizzy Gillespie, Charlie Parker, bassist Charles Mingus, and drummer Max Roach. It was called "The Greatest Jazz Concert Ever," and it was, very fortunately for the public, recorded by Charles Mingus. The bad news for the musicians was that their paychecks for the concert bounced. The men never got a penny for the recording, either. Mingus gave the tape to his wife in a divorce settlement.

By the mid-1950s, Bud was hospitalized again. After his release at the end of the decade, he and Buttercup (with whom he had a son, John) went to Paris. There the jazz world loved his music, and people knew they had to try to keep him away from alcohol. American musicians who heard him play when they visited Paris were astounded at times by how wonderful his music still was. Then there were days when his mental and physical deterioration became plain in his work. He almost always sounded magnificent on his recordings from the late 1940s and early 1950s. After that, his powers kept diminishing.

In the early 1960s, he contracted tuberculosis. A French jazz fan named Francis Poudras became his great friend and accompanied him to the United States in 1964. Bud was supposedly better by then. Reporters asked him what he was looking forward to most in his own country. He said, "Handling my own dough."[17] He played at Birdland, where his performances were erratic—soaring and magnificent one night, and uninspired, with his hands failing him, the next night. He still wasn't given his own money, because it was feared he would spend it on alcohol.

Bud wandered away from his guardian several times. Once he walked all the way across the Bronx to the apartment of Elmo Hope and his wife, Bertha, also a pianist. Bud was so exhausted that he couldn't do anything. Bertha kept offering him water or juice. But he refused everything and spent two hours trying to catch his breath. Bertha thought he might still have had tuberculosis. Finally she called Nellie Monk, who was one of the people looking for Bud that day.[18] He actually didn't have much longer to live. Francis Poudras went back to Paris without Bud, and Bud went to live in Brooklyn. He died in 1966, primarily of the results of alcoholism and neglect of his conditions.

The Piano Tree

This outline focuses on the pivotal jazz pianists throughout the twentieth century. Some have been innovators, and some have been virtuosos; all have set standards for other pianists.

From 1900 to 1918

The most popular music in the United States was ragtime. The most famous ragtime pianist and composer was **Scott Joplin,** whose best-known song was "Maple Leaf Rag." Ragtime is syncopated, two-beat music that combines European-influenced melodies and harmonies with syncopated, African-derived rhythms.

From 1900 to the 1920s

Jelly Roll Morton and other pianists played syncopated music, too, including ragtime, ethnic music, particularly the blues, and American musical theater and pop songs, church music, and spirituals. New Orleans–born Morton, who called himself the first true jazz pianist, played in a drawling, flowing, rhythmic style with looser rhythms and less decorations than ragtime had.

Jelly Roll Morton

From the 1900s to the 1930s

James P. Johnson

In Harlem, stride pianists played music related to early jazz in New Orleans, but stride was faster and often brighter and more urbane, with greater European influence. Stride players were often soloists, playing melody, harmony, and rhythm by themselves. Among the greatest Harlem stride pianists were *James P. Johnson, Willie "the Lion" Smith, Luckey Roberts,* and, best of all, Johnson's protégé, stride pianist and composer *Fats Waller,* who wrote "Ain't Misbehavin'."

Willie "the Lion" Smith

1920s *Art Tatum,* a blind pianist well known in his native Columbus, Ohio, in the 1920s, arrived in New York in 1931. Fats Waller called Tatum "God." Tatum's left hand played complicated stride rhythms while his right hand played very difficult, light, swift, extended improvisations guided by his brilliant understanding of harmonies.

1925 *Earl Hines,* a fine jazz pianist, met Louis Armstrong in Chicago, where they played and recorded together. Hines developed a "trumpet style" of playing long, flowing lines with his right hand. He became recognized for his contribution to the foundation of the art of modern jazz piano playing. By the end of the decade, leading a band in Chicago's Grand Terrace Ballroom, he broadcast coast to coast on radio, influencing young pianists everywhere.

1927 *Duke Ellington* took his big band into Harlem's glamorous Cotton Club in New York and began to compose music inspired by and tailored to the strengths of his musicians. He became the greatest jazz composer in his era—some say the greatest in jazz history—and one of the most important American composers.

Art Tatum

1930s

Count Basie led his band in Kansas City, Missouri, *Mary Lou Williams* toured with a swing-era band led by Andy Kirk, and *Teddy Wilson* played with many important bands in Chicago and New York. These three were among the most distinctive players of jazz piano. Basie pared down the stride style and played extraordinarily effective, one-note lines with an impeccable sense of swing. Williams composed and arranged. And Teddy Wilson had a clarity of style, with a delightful, light touch. Wilson learned from Earl Hines and added his own ideas for harmonies and improvisation with long, melodic lines. Wilson, an African-American, joined white clarinetist Benny Goodman's integrated trio with white drummer Gene Krupa. Later they played in the Benny Goodman Quartet with African-American vibraphon-

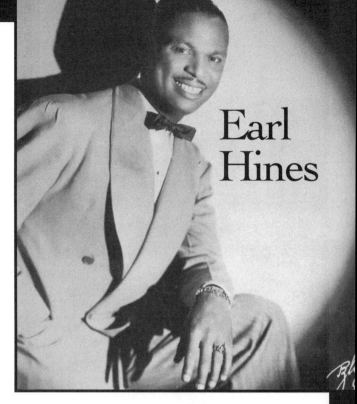

Earl Hines

Count Basie

ist Lionel Hampton. The success of the integrated group proved to be a milestone in jazz.

Mary Lou Williams

Jay McShann, an Oklahoma-born, Kansas City–based, blues-rooted pianist and bandleader, hired bebop innovator Charlie "Bird" Parker. McShann's earliest education came from listening to Hines on radio. Later McShann hung out with Art Tatum, who loved to play all night in after-hours clubs. McShann eventually went to college to study music formally.

Pianist and composer *Irene Wilson,* who had led her own groups in Chicago, moved with her husband Teddy Wilson to New York City. Irene wrote many outstanding popular songs admired by jazz musicians.

From the 1930s to the 1940s

In the swing era's big bands, which were very popular until the late 1940s, pianists had to adapt to the needs of the larger group. Basing their techniques on Hines's style, they discovered they had more freedom than ever to explore the harmonies and melodies of songs, and they became better improvisers. Bassists and drummers took over the rhythmic work that stride pianists had done with their left hands. A pianist, bassist, and drummer together, sometimes with a guitarist, were called a rhythm section.

Milt Buckner, studying Hines, developed a "locked hands" style of playing (that Hines also used) to make himself heard well in the midst of a loud big band.

1940s

Nat "King" Cole, learning from Earl Hines's style, became a world-famous trio leader. He played with a great sense of swing and harmonic sophistication. The beboppers extended the earlier development of jazz during the Jazz Age and the big band and swing eras. Among the bebop pianists, the most important were Thelonious Monk and Bud Powell.

Thelonious Monk started out playing stride piano in New York. When Mary Lou Williams settled in town, Monk learned more styles by playing with her. He began experimenting with harmonies and developed an eccentric style that marked him as one of the most important early bebop innovators. Monk's compositions, such as "Round Midnight," ranked as the best, most influential in jazz after Duke Ellington's. Even trumpeter Dizzy Gillespie copied Monk's piano style exactly and always played

Monk's songs. Though Monk had severe psychological problems, he managed to encourage and teach younger musicians.

Bud Powell, a fiery soloist, learned from Williams and Monk. He became an extremely popular, influential bebop pianist. He died young in the 1960s, a victim of his own mental problems and self-neglect, and at a time when Monk, long overlooked by the public, was finally winning public acclaim.

Dorothy Donegan, born in Chicago, became recognized as an exceptional jazz pianist. She went to Hollywood to star in films and instead launched a career in clubs and concert halls. She then toured worldwide. She played traditional jazz, boogie-woogie, and classical pieces for decades.

Hank Jones, a great swing-era pianist, worked his way across the country from Pontiac, Michigan, joined a group led by well-known trumpeter Oran "Hot Lips" Page in New York, and went on to develop into one of the most important jazz stylists. Younger pianists showed up for his performances year after year to take lessons from his touch and harmonic sense.

Algerian-born jazz pianist *Martial Solal* settled in Paris and wrote scores for movies. He found himself acclaimed for his vibrant style and became an international jazz star.

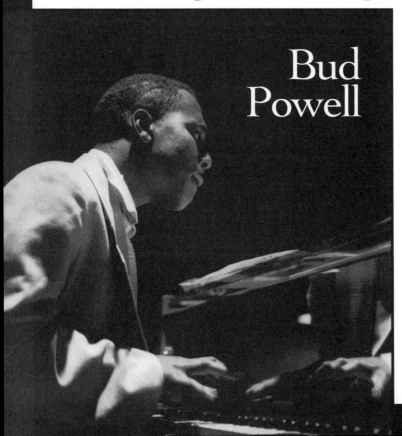

Bud
Powell

After 1945

Toshiko Akiyoshi, born in Manchuria, studied in Tokyo, where she fell under the spell of Teddy Wilson's recordings and learned to play jazz by ear. She also loved Bud Powell's recordings. Eventually she moved to the United States at the urging of American jazz musicians. First she studied at the Berklee College of Music in Boston, then she formed her own prize-winning big band, for which she composes and arranges. She also leads small groups.

George Shearing

1950s

Erroll Garner, composer of "Misty," became a very popular composer and stylist. He had a swinging, rolling, forceful style, which appealed to many people. *Jimmy Rowles,* like Hank Jones, became a role model for young pianists because of his touch and harmonic sophistication. As an accompanist, Rowles worked with Billie Holiday, Ella Fitzgerald, Sarah Vaughan, and others.

British-born, classically trained, blind jazz pianist *George Shearing* first arrived in the United States in the 1940s and struggled for attention. In the 1950s, he founded the George Shearing Quintet and with it achieved fame and fortune. He played with the "locked hands" style that he picked up from recordings of Milt Buckner. Shearing composed the jazz classic "Lullaby of Birdland."

From the 1950s to the 1960s

Great stylists and interesting composers emerged from among the jazz pianists. They helped to define the sound of jazz in the decade after the bebop revolution. Jazz was fragmenting and diversifying into factions or styles. Everyone experimented.

Among the composers was **Bobby Timmons,** who wrote "Moanin'." In 1968, he was the first jazz musician to receive a grant from the National Endowment for the Arts (NEA). **Horace Silver** wrote tunes such as "Señor Blues" and "Song for My Father," which became nationwide hits. Critics called Timmons and Silver "hard boppers" for their focus on the blues roots of jazz.

Joe Zawinul, pianist in a popular group led by alto saxophonist Julian "Cannonball" Adderley, composed "Mercy, Mercy, Mercy," a song steeped in blues feeling.

Lennie Tristano, a blind, East Coast pianist, started his own school. His teaching emphasized a cool, even coldsounding, version of the intense, sometimes fiery and aggressive bebop style.

Classically trained **John Lewis** became the pianist in the exceptionally popular Modern Jazz Quartet. The Quartet was known as a "Third Stream" group because of its emphasis on European influences.

From the late 1950s through the 1960s

Bill Evans

Miles Davis, one of the most influential jazz musicians, led innovative acoustic jazz groups that included excellent pianists. Davis used modes, or themes, rather than chords as the basis for his improvisations.

The first pianist in Davis's group was tradition-oriented *Red Garland.* Next was *Bill Evans,* generally regarded as the most important modern acoustic jazz piano innovator. Evans started his own trio in 1959 and created a romantic, sensitive, introspective style—an impressionistic lyricism—by using lush harmonies and long, mode-based improvisations. This style introduced new textures into the jazz language.

The pianists who followed Evans in Davis's group were, in order, *Wynton Kelly,* who died young, *Herbie Hancock,*

Chick Corea, Keith Jarrett, and Joe Zawinul. All were respected by their peers and, after leaving Davis, went on to have distinguished careers. Hancock, Corea, and Jarrett reached pinnacles of success as mainstream acoustic pianists and branched out to other fields of music. Hancock and Corea played and composed rock and jazz/rock fusion music. They emphasized work with electronic instruments during the reign of rock music in the 1960s and 1970s. They also toured together, performing in an acoustic piano duo for concerts.

Jarrett became famous for improvisatory music, particularly for his Köln Concert. By reputation he follows the avant garde or free jazz style. Zawinul founded a very popular rock/jazz fusion band called Weather Report. His music has a closer relationship to rock than to jazz, and he came to concentrate on experiments with electronic music.

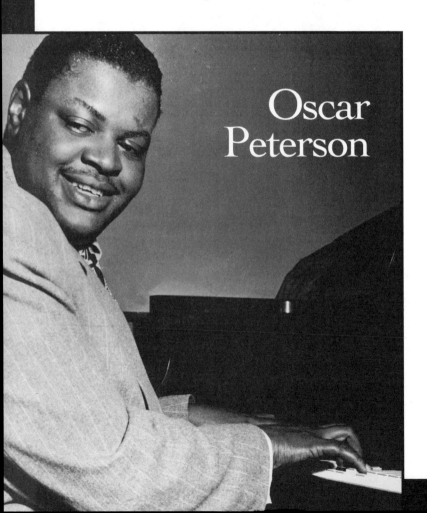

Oscar
Peterson

From the 1950s to the 1990s

Cecil Taylor

In 1951, pianist *Dave Brubeck* launched a very popular quartet noted for its cool blend of European music with jazz. Brubeck liked to play two entirely different rhythms simultaneously, one with each hand. His great alto saxophonist Paul Desmond, who composed the well-known "Take Five," supplied the quartet's airy, flowing sound especially revered by college students. Canadian-born *Oscar Peterson* emerged as the heir apparent to Art Tatum when entrepreneur and jazz concert producer Norman Granz became Peterson's manager. Granz gave Peterson's fast, articulate style world exposure. Peterson based his illustrious trio on the Nat "King" Cole trio's instrumentation of piano, bass, and guitar and became the highest-paid jazz pianist in jazz history. Though some critics would call his style cold for its technical perfection, Peterson nevertheless stands out as one of the most talented, dazzling players in all of jazz.

Cecil Taylor became the leading iconoclast of jazz piano. He played atonal, wild music. After analyzing music written and performed by jazz and European classical musicians, he decided to pull traditional music apart and play the opposite. In doing this, he turned himself into a remarkable innovator. Critics called him a free jazz player.

Though he had almost no commercial success in terms of audience appeal for most of his career, Taylor's creativity attracted supporters. he found teaching positions and was awarded grants, including the vaunted MacArthur Award—the so-called "genius award." In the 1990s, he found wider acceptance with audiences and starred at the commercially oriented club The Village Vanguard.

McCoy
Tyner

From the 1960s

Jazz's commercial appeal was eclipsed by rock music. That loud, elemental music drowned out the acoustic pianists. These dedicated musicians, though, continued to try to develop their art in jazz clubs and lofts or in private homes. *McCoy Tyner* played the piano in legendary saxophonist John Coltrane's group, which critics said played "sheets of sound," so dense was the music.

McCoy went on to lead his own successful group, continuing to play as an heir to Coltrane, with the piano cast in a percussive as well as harmonic role. McCoy's exciting music influenced many young pianists to pursue careers in jazz.

Among the other important free jazz pianists and composers have been *Joanne Brackeen, Don Pullen, Paul Bley, Richie Beirach, Keith Jarrett, and Michele Rosewoman.* Most have had either NEA or Meet the Composer grants, or both.

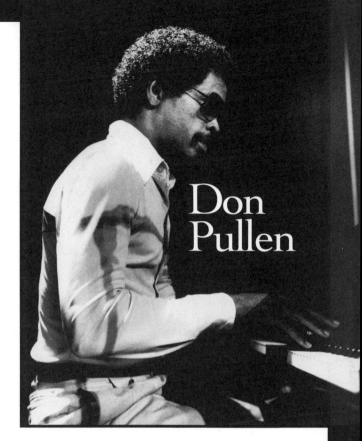

Don Pullen

The 1980s and 1990s

During a renaissance of the public's interest in jazz, many young experimentalists began to flourish. That is, they found places, most notably a New York club called the Knitting Factory, where they could play for audiences interested in music on the cutting edge. Even in mainstream jazz clubs and concerts, audiences became receptive to odder harmonies and more sophisticated music than they had liked in the 1960s and 1970s.

Among the tradition-rooted jazz pianists in the limelight during

Kenny Barron

the last two decades of the twentieth century have been many who survived the rock era and spent those years gaining experience and polish. They now rank among the best jazz pianists ever—bebop authority *Barry Harris*, *Kenny Barron*, *John Hicks*, *Cedar Walton*, *Kirk Lightsey*, *Bill Mays*, *Roger Kellaway*, *Sir Roland Hanna*, *Tommy Flanagan*, *Dick Hyman*, *Adam Makovic*, and *Shirley Horne*, to name a few.

Younger pianists emerged, among them *Jim McNeeley*, *Mulgrew Miller*, *Billy Childs*, *Geri Allen*, *Renee Rosnes*, *Rachel Z*, *George Cables*, *Benny Green*, *Marcus Roberts*, *Kenny Kirkland*, *Danilo Perez*, *Kenny Drew Jr.*, *Cyrus Chestnut*, *Michael Weiss*, *Geoff Keezer*, *Mike Le-Donne*, experimentalist *Myra Melford*, and many others. They come not only from the United States but increasingly from all over, particularly Europe, Africa, Japan, and Central and South America.

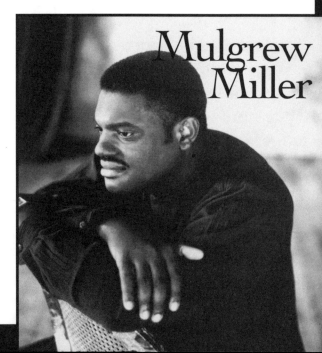

Mulgrew Miller

CHAPTER FIVE
Great Piano StyLists

No sooner had bebop become accepted by the general public as exciting new music than it spawned a wealth of new styles. All of them had their roots in bebop's sophistications and elaborations. Some musicians stressed the Latin influence that came into bebop through Dizzy's affinity for Latin music. Some musicians emphasized a driving, funky blues sound, which was called hard bop. Bobby Timmons and Horace Silver were called hard bop pianists, because their music stressed the soulful blues roots of jazz.

Timmons wrote a moving, poignant blues-based song, "Moanin'," about having the blues morning and night; it had a great vogue beginning in the 1950s. In 1968, he was the first musician to receive a National Endowment for the Arts grant. Unfortunately, he died young. Horace Silver had a series of hit tunes, such as "Song for My Father" and "Señor Blues." Though he had several health problems, Silver took excellent

The Modern Jazz Quartet became prominent in the 1950s, with John Lewis at the piano, Percy Heath on bass, Connie Kay on drums, and Milt Jackson at the vibraharps. The group blended jazz and European influences.

care of himself. People who knew him well said he never took a cigarette or a drink in his life.

Joe Zawinul, the pianist in saxophonist Cannonball Adderley's much-loved group, wrote a blues-drenched tune called "Mercy, Mercy, Mercy." With that, Cannonball's group became very famous. A European-born pianist, Zawinul was one of the keyboard players who left acoustic music and went on to experiment with electric instruments in fusion jazz groups.

Other musicians on the West Coast went in still another direction. Bebop had been an intense music; on the West Coast, musicians fell in love with a cool, laid-back sound. Baritone saxophonist Gerry Mulligan, who formed one of the most important groups in California, toyed with the idea of using a pianist, Jimmy Rowles, but then went ahead with a pianoless quartet. The music seemed to reflect the calm, tranquil, easeful feeling of California's topography, with its palm trees, warm weather, bright sun, beaches, and casual culture.

On the East Coast, a blind pianist named Lennie Tristano started his own cool "school." His students and protégés played a very cool, even cold-sounding version of bebop-rooted jazz.

And a Third Stream movement developed. Third Stream musicians, as they were dubbed, emphasized the importance of classical European music; they fused jazz and European music into chamber jazz—music with the civility of a string quartet and the swing and excitement of jazz. The leading Third Stream group was the Modern Jazz Quartet, founded in the early 1950s. Its members were pianist John Lewis, with a solid European classical education and an especially light touch, and his swinging sidemen, vibes player Milt Jackson, bassist Percy Heath, and drummer Connie Kay. Milt Jackson's trio actually had been the foundation on which the Modern Jazz Quartet was built. Its earliest records electrified audiences with their calm, cool, collected swing and an almost ethereal, otherworldly sound.

George Shearing's quintet and Ahmad Jamal's trio in the 1950s had a similar effect on the public. Their music was simultaneously exciting, swinging, entertaining, and soothing. Pianist Stan Kenton led a band that tried to experiment with bebop; it featured a European influence, a

Striders, Beboppers and Beyond

somber trombone section, and Latin percussion. Though critics said his band didn't swing, with its heavy, intense, modern sound, Kenton had big hits with such tunes as "Artistry in Rhythm" and "The Peanut Vendor," and he won many awards.

Pianist Dave Brubeck also led a quartet emphasizing a cool blend of European music with jazz, from 1951 to the end of the 1960s. The group included a light, fluid alto saxophone played by Paul Desmond. Desmond made the group swing. Brubeck's other greatest asset was his rhythmic innovation. He was fond of playing two entirely different rhythms with each of his hands at the same time. The public liked the effect, and he launched a very popular career, overcoming the criticism of his heavy-handed touch.

Still another pianist, Erroll Garner, developed such an individualistic sound that he became uncategorizable. He was influenced by every style of jazz piano—ragtime, stride, swing, and bebop. With his right hand, he embellished songs in bebop fashion, but he never let go of the melodies of songs as they were written. The melodies were the things he had fallen in love with playing in the first place. Most of all, Garner was known for his romanticism. He played tremolo chords that had the warmth of a singer's vibrato, and his runs and arpeggiated chords could often sound like the passionate cries of lovers. Most effective of all were his strummed left-hand chords. He played the notes one after the other—but very quickly, for a rocking, bouncing, syncopated feeling—while his right hand played pretty melodies.

One day, as he was traveling on an airplane, he seemed to be singing, or talking, or humming to himself. There was an air of distress or deep concentration about him. A person in the next seat asked him if he felt all right. Garner said he was fine. In his head, he was composing his song, "Misty," which became one of the most popular and enduring standards. Even if Garner's name didn't become known to everyone, "Misty" became a household word, and most people learned to recognize his rhythmically idiosyncratic, inspired piano style instantly. Garner had his own heady brew of a distilled jazz style, which belonged to no school of thought but his own.

All the directions jazz took had their roots in bebop, and all the musicians built on the ideas of Dizzy, Bird, Monk, Bud, Clarke, and Roach and their followers.

Some musicians began to experiment with harmonies based on the music of foreign and ancient cultures. They left behind the scale upon which western music was based and used an ancient form of music called modes. Melodies and harmonies were built upon modal themes—phrases of several notes—instead of chords. The goal of all these experiments was to expand the vocabulary of the jazz language.

At the same time, many pianists simply kept working with the jazz language as it had been developed in the swing and bebop eras. Dorothy Donegan, a Chicago-born pianist, became so respected that she was invited to go to Hollywood and make a film. She played in clubs on the West Coast and married a club owner; by the 1950s, he was managing her career and helped book her in the Embers, a prestigious, glamorous New York City supper club. He personally guaranteed that he would pay the Embers's owner if Dorothy's group failed to attract customers and lost money for the club during her engagement. She was a great success, played there for a long time, and returned often.

Keeping herself abreast of the latest trends and innovations, Marian McPartland took her group into the Hickory House, another prominent New York City club, and played there in the 1960s. Her reputation kept growing. She and Dorothy would be considered the grand ladies of jazz piano by the 1980s and 1990s.

In Chicago, pianists Junior Mance and Norman Simmons heard Bud Powell's music and became inspired at the start of their careers in the late 1940s and early 1950s. Mance played with singer Dinah Washington and bandleader Dizzy Gillespie before launching his own career as a leader of small groups. With his strong blues foundation, he made an impression on audiences. A piano-playing hero in a French movie, when asked what he dreamed about achieving in life, said he wanted to play like Junior Mance. In the 1990s, Mance joined Lionel Hampton's group, The Golden Men of Jazz, which had star billing all around the world.

Striders to Beboppers and Beyond

Norman Simmons also had a strong blues underpinning. He developed into one of the finest accompanists for jazz singers, working for Carmen McRae, Joe Williams, and many others. In the 1990s, he has accompanied Kevin Mahogany, an accomplished musician and budding star who seems destined to carry the torch of jazz singing into the twenty-first century.

Billy Taylor also started a distinguished career in the 1940s, in awe of Tatum, Hines, and Powell. He developed into an important jazz educator and a spokesman from the jazz community to the federal government. In the 1980s, he began appearing regularly on a CBS-TV show, "Sunday Morning," presenting jazz guests.

Versatile Ray Bryant, with a rhythmic gift he began developing in his family's Pentecostal church, became known as a blues pianist and signed a contract to record with Columbia. He also had a lean, swinging, sophisticated approach to jazz standards. Many a schmaltzy or saccharine pop tune was rescued from its own weaknesses by Ray's keen musicality and imagination. He knew exactly what to leave out and what to emphasize and add.

Oscar Peterson was hailed as the heir apparent to Art Tatum. Born in Montreal to a West Indian family, Peterson caught the ear of jazz concert and record producer Norman Granz. Granz was the founder of Jazz at the Philharmonic, a concert series that took jazz artists on tours to major cities around the country. In the 1950s, Granz began managing Peterson and giving him the exposure that made his fast, articulate style world famous. Peterson led peerless piano-bass-guitar trios inspired by Nat King Cole. And with his group and his manager as his platform, Peterson launched himself to stardom as the highest-paid jazz pianist in history.

These are only a few of the great interpretive pianists of the post-bebop era. It was a time when the scene was bountifully endowed with pianists who loved the jazz tradition founded on swing and bebop. They established their own classy, exciting, interpretive styles. Many of these players were virtuosos and crowd pleasers, even if they were not innovators. Some of them communicated better with the public than the innovators did.

100

CHAPTER SIX

The Pianists in Miles Davis's Groups

Trumpeter Miles Davis, one of the most influential jazz musicians who ever lived, constantly evolved. He began his career in New York under the wings of the fiery beboppers, Bird and Dizzy, in the 1940s. Miles loved Monk's playing, too; by the 1950s, Miles developed a unique sound based on his haunting, eerie tone. Its coolness inspired the West Coast musicians. But for his intensity and deep feeling, Miles clearly represented the East Coast as well—or more accurately both coasts and the entire country in between. He became the leading jazz musician of his era. A British jazz critic called Miles's music "the sound of loneliness."[1]

This sound mirrored the isolation people were beginning to feel after World War II. The United States had not suffered the devastation of the war firsthand, but American society was in a state of flux. Families were uprooted, moving away from each other to study and work. And values were changing, as people struck out independently. The cult of the individual began to grow in earnest. Self-realization became a goal in itself.

As social values underwent a virtual revolution, the laws of the country started changing to accommodate the economic, political, and social realities of Americans. Miles's music was not only musically advanced; it interpreted the pensive mood of the country and penetrated to the hearts of audiences. They felt a spiritual kinship with Miles's self-expression.

Miles hired some of the most important piano stylists in the history of the art. He recorded with Horace Silver, John Lewis, and Thelonious Monk. His career as a jazz leader started in force in 1955, when he formed a quintet including pianist Red Garland. With his percussive approach and lyrical right hand lines influenced by Bud Powell, Garland excelled as an accompanist for Miles. Garland played for Miles's album, *Milestones*, which ventured into the concept of modal playing, improvising on scale patterns of a few notes instead of chord changes.

A mode is a sequence of notes in a given whole-step, half-step pattern that establishes a tonality—an overall, dominant feeling or keynote. Modes weren't new. They had been used in ancient Greek and modern European music. But jazz musicians used them to gain freedom from chords. Miles Davis said he felt jazz compositions were becoming "thick with chords," and he wanted to emphasize melody—a modal or scalar melody—as the jumping off point for a musician's imagination and improvisations.

Bill Evans

In 1958, Red Garland left to lead his own trio. Miles hired pianist Bill Evans for a sextet including two great saxophonists, John Coltrane and Cannonball Adderley, with bassist Paul Chambers and drummer Jimmy Cobb—all rising musicians. The group recorded *Kind of Blue*, one of the most influential modern jazz albums in the post-bebop era. Their music had a haunting beauty, which its soloists achieved by improvising on modes and tonal centers instead of chords. Bill Evans brought his deep love of the French Impressionist composers Claude Debussy and Maurice Ravel to rise to the challenge of Miles's music. Under their spell, Evans was beginning to introduce new textures to the jazz piano language.

Evans stayed with Miles for about six months, then began working with his own trio in 1959 as the warm-up group for Benny Goodman in Basin Street, a famous New York jazz club. That's where Evans first played with bassist Scott LaFaro and drummer Paul Motian. They were the right people to help Evans develop. Evans created a romantic, sensitive, introspective style—an impressionistic lyricism—by using lush harmonies and long, mode-based improvisations.

For his chords, he played notes that the chords of a written song might suggest. But the notes weren't necessarily the root notes of the chords that had been written for songs. And the chords that he played suggested not only the notes of the original chords but many other chords as well. So the direction he took was never clearly defined or ordained. He could go in the direction of the root of the chord or on to an entirely new chord. Pianists said he found new voicings for chords. Primarily for his work with harmonies and for his exquisite touch on the piano keys, he was considered the most innovative and influential pianist since Thelonious Monk and Bud Powell.

Most pianists, even those who began their careers before Powell came on the scene, integrated Evans's ideas into their styles. Pianists younger than Evans often fell under his spell completely. Among them were modernists who could play with Evans's sophistication but who floundered when asked to accompany a group in a swing-era, blues-based, or big band repertoire. And the youngsters enamored of Evans had to study the long history of jazz piano's development before they could sustain careers as jazz pianists.

Born on August 16, 1929 in Plainfield, New Jersey, Evans studied piano as a boy, went on to flute and violin, played in his own band with his brother, and attended Southeastern Louisiana University with a flute scholarship. During the summers, he worked with other emerging bebop musicians, and he played in a band before serving three years in the

Army. Musicians who knew him in those days thought he was talented but had no exceptional style of his own.

Returning to New York in 1954, he described his own style as open and physical. He felt threatened by the big city, and he responded to its size and impersonality by playing aggressively. Around this time, he met pianist/band leader George Russell, who was devoting himself to modal music. Evans made a recording called "All About Rosie" with Russell, which was widely praised. Suddenly the critics described Evans as one of the best young jazz pianists. A few years later, after recording the album *Kind of Blue* with Miles as leader, Evans was launched in an important career.

In 1958, he won a *Down Beat* magazine critics poll. He would win again four more times, and he would also receive five Grammy awards from the National Academy of Recording Arts and Sciences. More honors came to him from Europe, England, and Japan.

His style reached maturity in his trio with LaFaro and Motian. They played with such communion that they sounded like one instrument. On such songs as "Autumn Leaves" and Evans's own song, "Waltz for Debbie," LaFaro and Motian interwove and interlocked their lines with spectacular success. The trio performed together often until June 1961, when they recorded *The Village Vanguard Sessions* for the Riverside label. Ten days later, Scott LaFaro was killed in a car crash. For a while, Evans was inconsolable.

Eventually, friends encouraged him to play again. Critics wrote about the colors of Evans's playing. Audiences experienced his music as romantic and pensive moods. Though he could swing and play brightly, too, he was best known for his introspective sound. As a soloist, he was spellbinding, and he recorded solo performances that are considered jazz classics.

A thoroughgoing child of the bebop era, Evans fell victim to a heroin addiction and never broke his habit. It led him to self neglect and social failures; he had pitifully little control over his finances. During the 1970s, he sometimes performed at New York's foremost piano-bass jazz club, Bradley's, owned by jazz lover Bradley Cunningham. (Bradley often lent money to Evans, and Evans always paid it back.) In September 1980, Evans died from a bleeding ulcer. At the time he was separated from his wife, his son Evan, and an adopted daughter.

Marian McPartland, upon learning of Evans's death, said, "You know how people used to speak about Art Tatum in hushed tones. I think people will speak of Bill Evans in hushed tones for even longer."[2] Evans's lawyer sent Bradley Cunningham a letter saying that Bill had died still owing Bradley money. Would Bradley accept about fifty cents on the dollar as repayment from the estate? Bradley replied that he would accept the letter itself as repayment.

Wynton Kelly

Evans was replaced in Miles's group by Wynton Kelly. Born in Jamaica, the West Indies, in December 1931, Wynton moved to Brooklyn as a child with his family and began playing in rhythm and blues bands. His horizons were defined by Bud Powell, and his playing attracted the attention of very important instrumentalists and singers. He replaced Evans in 1959, working with bassist Paul Chambers and drummer Jimmy Cobb.

Kelly and Chambers left Miles in 1963; Cobb soon followed them. The trio worked as a group on their own, with legendary guitarist Wes Montgomery, and with guest saxophonists for a Baltimore music society. When Wes formed a group with his brothers, the Kelly-Chambers-Cobb rhythm section stayed together. But Wynton Kelly developed epilepsy. Jimmy Cobb, his close friend, thought the illness was probably caused by Wynton's excessive drinking. Whenever Jimmy visited Wynton in a jazz bar near Wynton's apartment, Wynton had many drinks lined up in front of him. His friends and admirers kept buying them. Several times on the road, Cobb helped the young pianist through seizures.[3]

One afternoon, having arrived in a city to play a date, the rhythm section went out for a walk to relax. As they were turning back toward their hotel, Kelly kept walking straight, in the midst of a seizure. Cobb took him upstairs and helped him through the night. "The next day, Kelly played the job as if there wasn't a thing in the world wrong," Cobb recalled.[4] Cobb knew that Kelly's body ached after his seizure. It was a miracle that he could play so well. He was both an adept accompanist and a powerful, rhythmically gifted soloist. Despite his illness, he worked until the day he died, during a tour in Toronto, Canada, in 1971, when he was thirty-nine years old.

Herbie Hancock

Wynton Kelly influenced pianist Herbie Hancock, who went into Miles Davis's group in 1963. Born in Chicago on April 12, 1940, Herbie began studying piano at a very early age. A prodigy, he performed the first movement of a Mozart concerto as a guest soloist with the Chicago Symphony Orchestra, in a special project for talented young musicians, when he was eleven. He practiced for that performance on a piano with broken keys; his family had found it in a church cellar on Chicago's South Side.

Herbie was familiar with arrangements by some of the leading jazz arrangers for orchestras. He wanted to become a professional musician, but his mother insisted that he attend Grinnell College and aim for a secure career as an engineer. Once in school, he switched to a music major. By 1960, he was playing in clubs occasionally with a great saxophonist, Coleman Hawkins. A well-known trumpeter invited Herbie to go to New York City and make a recording as a sideman on the Blue Note label. Hancock made such a good impression that he was offered his own record date in May 1962.

On his album, he included his catchy, danceable composition, "Watermelon Man," with a strong rhythm and blues underpinning. A Latin percussionist, Mongo Santamaria, made the first hit recording of the tune. Hancock paid his bills for several years with the proceeds from that composition. And Miles Davis invited the young wizard to work in a quintet that included bassist Ron Carter and drummer Tony Williams—a famous, modern rhythm section.

Hancock benefited from the exposure, and Miles benefited from Hancock's versatility and adaptability, his understanding of harmony and rhythm-section playing. At Miles's request, Herbie began playing synthesizers as well as acoustic piano. He also composed songs which became jazz standards—"Maiden Voyage," "Dolphin Dance," "The Sorcerer," and "Speak Like a Child." They became titles for his own excellent, popular jazz albums.

Herbie's time with Miles was filled with lessons. "One time Miles noticed that I was in a sort of rut and disgusted with my playing. And so I said, 'Miles, sometimes I just don't know what to play.' Miles said, 'Then don't play nothing.' " A gleeful smile crossed Hancock's face at the memory. "Silence is important in music. You don't have to play all the time. I'm not a drummer. I'm a piano player."[5]

Another night, Miles leaned over to Herbie during a club date and said, "Don't play the butter notes." Hancock had no idea what Miles meant. "You had to figure out what he said sometimes, first of all because of his whispery voice and because he liked to be provocative. Maybe what he meant was: play the ornaments, don't play the description—the notes that obviously describe the chords. And keep the music buoyant, mysterious and ethereal." Miles made Hancock think for himself and find the best way to go.

Returning from his honeymoon in Brazil in 1968, Hancock discovered that he had been replaced by Chick Corea in the Davis quintet. At first shocked and devastated, worried about supporting his new family, Hancock began leading his own group, which combined elements of jazz, rock, and electric instruments and devices. Intrigued and successful with his fusion group, Hancock expanded his involvement with all kinds of synthesizers. His 1973 album *Headhunters* was a commercial success, containing a hit tune, "Chameleon."

Striders to Beboppers and Beyond

Establishing himself in Los Angeles, playing occasionally with the critically praised acoustic group VSOP, Hancock became a successful West Coast musician. His single "Rockit" in 1983 reached number one on the pop chart. Undisputedly, he was as fine a player on electric instruments as nearly anybody has ever managed to become. Manufacturers gave him very expensive machines to test and use for his projects; electronics bewitched Hancock.

Critics accused him of deserting acoustic jazz in favor of funky fusion music, which was commercial. Herbie decided, "I think both jazz and pop are beautiful, or I wouldn't mess with it. Instead of critics trusting my judgment or at least opening up to the possibility that I could feel that [pop] music has value and is worth it, they say I'm into pop music just for the money. That's a very ignorant statement. It's ridiculous to say that pop is a get-rich-quick gimmick, a foolproof plan. If that were true, everybody would be a star. But critics just don't know the field. I have respect for the common man. I feel that people who may not have a trained ear for music—or for jazz—can in many cases feel something in music that eludes people who are trained in music or acclimated to jazz. Pop music lovers have a certain sensitivity."

He wanted to write scores for films, for the artistic challenges and financial rewards, but did not find doors springing open for him. Then he got the chance to write the score for the 1986 jazz film *Round Midnight* starring Dexter Gordon. Herbie also played piano in that film and looked clean-cut and sane behind Dexter, who portrayed a deeply troubled saxophonist. Herbie won an Oscar for the soundtrack to the movie.

There have been many awards and gold records in his career, as he has moved adeptly back and forth from jazz to popular music, films, concerts, and clubs as a composer, arranger, and performer. After he won the Oscar for *Round Midnight*, Herbie's career surged ahead even farther. He began touring with famous acoustic jazz musicians, some of whom he had worked with in Miles's groups, in Europe, the United States, and Japan. Projects came easily from then on.

Chick Corea and Herbie Hancock toured together with a fusion group in 1988, their first collaboration since 1978. Two of the great modernists who played with Miles Davis, they have established eclectic careers in jazz and popular music.

Younger pianists such as Geri Allen regarded Hancock as one of the best, most successful, and enviable modern jazz pianists. He lived with his wife and family in a brilliantly verdant, palm-tree-lined street on the border of Beverly Hills. In one of the upstairs rooms was a Buddhist shrine, which Herbie had installed for his private meditation. While pop music fans enjoyed his work, veteran jazz critics were overjoyed at his increased involvement with acoustic jazz.

Chick Corea

Armando "Chick" Corea Jr., who was born in Chelsea, Massachusetts, near Boston, began playing piano as a child. Tutored by his father, a bandleader and trumpeter, Chick listened to the bebop founders, including Bud Powell, and hard bop pianist Horace Silver. Chick played with local musicians, including a Latin band, and felt a deep affinity for Latin rhythms. In 1959, he went to New York to study for a liberal arts degree at Columbia University. But he made up his mind quickly to leave college when he heard Miles Davis play at Birdland. The thrill of that experience sent Chick home to Boston to practice and prepare for an audition at the Juilliard School of Music in New York. He was accepted at that prestigious school for classical music. But he quickly became restless, because he wanted to improvise music; he left school to work with Latin bands in town.

His first important professional job was with Mongo Santamaria in 1962. Then he went to Willie Bobo's Latin band and after that to flutist Herbie Mann's group, which also emphasized Latin music. Chick also played with Blue Mitchell, a trumpeter and one of the musicians whose work Chick had studied on recordings years earlier. From all his experience and inclinations, Chick developed as a hard bop pianist with a crisp and melodic style.

In 1966, he got the chance to record his own compositions on an album called *Tones For Joan's Bones*. (The music from this recording is also on a later compilation called *Inner Space*.) Among the pianists he had studied and admired were Bill Evans, Herbie Hancock, and McCoy Tyner. Tyner had been gaining wide exposure in saxophonist John Coltrane's modally oriented group in the early 1960s. On Chick's own albums, including *Now He Sings, Now He Sobs*, done in 1968, his characteristically articulate and searching style began to emerge. He could play very creatively and with exceptional speed.

That year, he had a call from drummer Tony Williams to join Miles Davis's group. Herbie Hancock had been delayed in Brazil on his honeymoon. Chick dropped everything to go to Miles's group to fill in for Hancock. Telephoning Miles beforehand to ask for instructions and set a rehearsal time, Chick was astonished when Miles said, "Play what you hear." There wasn't going to be a rehearsal. Miles liked to bring musicians together in a group, let them explore music, and build the group in action.

Chick showed up for the date and played the set's first song, "Agitation." It was aptly named for his debut. "I'll never forget it," he said. "The band took off like a rocket ship. It was like the shock of suddenly traveling 500 miles per hour. I just hung on. I knew they were playing tunes, but they had them so facile and abstracted that not even a musician's ear could tell what chord changes were going by. After the set I went up to the bar to buy myself a drink. Miles came up behind me and whispered in my ear, 'Chick, you're a mutha.' That was it! What more could I ask for?"[6]

Miles insisted that Chick play an electric piano for the group, as Herbie Hancock and even Bill Evans had done earlier. Chick resisted at first. Soon he found that he could infuse his playing on the usually impersonal-sounding instrument with warmth, lyricism, and personality. Chick was in awe of Miles, who was not only a brilliant musician but an observant and adaptable one. Many other jazz musicians felt simply helpless when loud, simple, rock music won over the public. The more sophisticated jazz became, the more the public turned to the elemental rock music. Miles decided to bring the two arts together, and he produced a jazz-rock fusion record, *Bitches Brew*, in 1969. Other jazz musicians didn't follow his example in a great crowd, but some did. They admired Miles for communicating with the public. He made a type of jazz commercially acceptable to audiences.

The following year, Corea and another musician in Miles's group, British-born bassist Dave Holland, decided to go out on their own and play improvisatory, experimental music. They became part of an interesting group called Circle, which made a few albums. But they attracted only small audiences intrigued by free jazz. It was experimental music which began to pull apart the traditions and principles of classic, mainstream, acoustic jazz. Chick liked improvising entire performances of experimental music on stage, using such techniques as plucked piano strings. But he didn't want to lead the life of a starving artist. "We were sending audiences up the river," he observed.[7]

In debt, he went back to Boston and played little jobs, until he met new musicians to work with, including a Brazilian percussionist and singer named Airto Moreira. Chick hired him for his new jazz fusion group, called Return To Forever. By "forever," he meant "spiritual awareness,"[8] and for him, spiritual awareness meant a connection with a large audience. As his group developed, the music, with a strong Latin underpinning, improved. Return To Forever's second album, *Light As a Feather*, included his impassioned composition, "Spain," a joyful, entertaining piece that jazz musicians as well as audiences loved. After that, Corea went full steam ahead into hard rock with high energy music played on electronic instruments.

Although there were critics who accepted his work with electronics, Corea himself finally broke up his group, saying it was dissolving into "a mushroom of uncontrollable sound."[9] He continued with experiments in electronic fusion, bringing in influences from classical Latin and Spanish music, utilizing violins and brass ensembles. And he continued as an acoustic pianist, too.

In 1978, he toured with Herbie Hancock for duo piano concerts, which were recorded and released as albums. Chick also made records with vibraphonist Gary Burton. On a piano built by a Scientologist, whom Chick met during his long association with the Church of Scientology, he recorded an album called *Delphi 1*, which runs the gamut from stride piano to free jazz. In 1981, he began a group, Trio Music, with Miroslav Vitous and Roy Haynes, and in 1985 established his Elektric Band, with an acoustic bassist and a drummer.

His performances are sold-out events. His style, no matter what he plays, is lucid and articulate. And his technique is the envy of other pianists.

Keith Jarrett

For his daring, Keith Jarrett became one of the best known pianists of the Hancock-Corea generation. Sometimes Jarrett played electric organ in Miles's band while Chick played electric piano. Then Jarrett took over all the keyboard work, outstaying Corea in the band for a little while. Jarrett had already become prominent in the jazz world as a member of a prestigious quartet led by saxophonist Charles Lloyd that emphasized improvisation.

Jarrett is best known for his solo concerts, which he began performing in 1972. He walked onstage and improvised two extended pieces of music, each about thirty to forty-five minutes long. Devoting himself solely to the acoustic piano, he achieved his greatest success as an improvisatory, unaccompanied, solo artist with *The Köln Concert* in Germany in 1975. His work remains eclectic; at times he has worked with jazz musicians in trios and quartets, particularly with bassist Gary Peacock and famed drummer Jack DeJohnette, and he has written for classical chamber groups and orchestras.

Herbie Hancock, Chick Corea, and Keith Jarrett can be thought of as a kind of triumvirate. All of them received exposure with Miles's groups. All exemplify the pinnacle of success for mainstream acoustic jazz pianists, although each has branched out.

Joe Zawinul

Another pianist who achieved fame as an electronic keyboards player and a composer is Joe Zawinul. Born in Vienna, Austria, on July 7, 1932, fated to grow up in war-torn Europe, his was a hectic, tragic childhood. He had a twin brother who died at the age of four. Zawinul has said that his family had little to eat. He sometimes stole food to help keep his family from starving under the Soviet occupation.

A gifted pianist, he began studying with classical musicians, attending the Vienna Conservatory, and playing a great variety of instruments in studio orchestras, cabarets, and for U.S. Army clubs. About jazz, he took his instruction by ear from recordings by clarinetist-singer Woody Herman and his band, pianist George Shearing, and others.

In 1959, Zawinul won a scholarship to the Berklee School of Music in Boston. Soon he began working with trumpeter Maynard Ferguson's big band. Then he switched to accompany singer Dinah Washington; he played electric piano for her biggest hit, "What a Diff'rence a Day Makes." His fortunes rose further when he became the pianist in saxophonist Julian "Cannonball" Adderley's exciting group from 1961 to 1970.

Miles Davis may have become impressed with the electric piano by listening to Zawinul; in the late 1960s and early 1970s, Zawinul played with Miles. In the mainstream jazz world, Zawinul is particularly revered for his composition "Mercy, Mercy, Mercy," on a recording led by Adderley with considerable commercial success, and for his composition "In a Silent Way," the title song for a classic fusion album by Miles.

With musicians who became his friends during his first decade in America, Zawinul founded a popular, jazz-rock fusion band, Weather Report. Its intense and sometimes spacey music has a far more obvious relationship to rock than jazz.

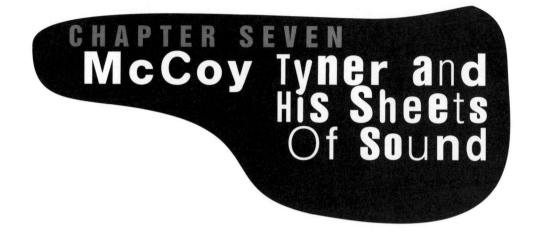

CHAPTER SEVEN

McCoy Tyner and His Sheets Of Sound

McCoy Tyner, a forceful pianist virtually the opposite of the subtle Bill Evans, went to work in saxophonist John Coltrane's group in 1960. Tyner, too, became influential. Some budding young musicians decided to become pianists when they heard McCoy play. Then they had to work their way back and find out about earlier artists, particularly Art Tatum, Earl Hines, Thelonious Monk, and Bud Powell. These were the same people, along with Ellington, who had inspired McCoy.

McCoy was born in Philadelphia, Pennsylvania, on December 11, 1938. His mother, a beauty shop owner, gave him a choice when he was thirteen. He could study singing or take piano lessons. He chose the piano, and he first played rhythm and blues, a popular, simpler music than jazz but a swinging one, too. Once McCoy became involved in music, it dominated his life. He practiced all the time. He also learned a lot from older Philadelphia jazz musicians, who introduced him to recordings by Charlie Parker, Miles Davis, and Bud Powell. "It was beautiful," McCoy recalled, "because I really got a chance to find out where the real music was."[1]

Not only did he hear Bud Powell on records, but for a while McCoy lived near Powell, whose family had a house near Philadelphia. Bud and his brother Richie occasionally played for Tyner and his buddies, some of whom would also become accomplished jazz musicians.

When McCoy was seventeen, in 1954, a friend introduced him to the most important influence of his early career: saxophonist John Coltrane. McCoy was playing with a band one day when Coltrane showed up to hear it. At the time, Coltrane was working as a sideman in Miles Davis's band. 'Trane, as he was called, had no regular group of his own. McCoy's first impression was that 'Trane was a very peaceful, humble man with a great deal of talent. He practiced constantly. Musicians who stayed in hotels with him saw him standing in stairwells, practicing for hours.

For the next five years, McCoy performed irregularly as a professional pianist at night and worked as a factory shipping clerk by day. When Coltrane occasionally hired a group, he called McCoy to play piano. In 1959, McCoy was offered a job as the pianist with a new group called the Jazztet, co-led by Art Farmer and Benny Golson, two very fine, established jazz horn players. McCoy stayed with them for six months, but his heart wasn't in the job. "John [Coltrane] was the only person I wanted to play with in those days," McCoy recalled.[2]

Coltrane finally decided to form his own group with Tyner, bassist Jimmy Garrison, and drummer Elvin Jones. Individually they were powerful players. Together they were dynamic, performing some of the loudest, most intense and impassioned music in jazz. Coltrane was experimenting with modes and vamps, or phrases, in which the piano played a prominently percussive as well as an harmonic role.

McCoy understood Coltrane's musical ideas very well, and he had a forceful touch and a thunderous and swinging drive that could rise to the occasion of accompanying Coltrane. McCoy's improvisations even resembled Coltrane's, as the saxophonist emphasized the spirituality of music; McCoy had become a Moslem in 1955 when he married a Moslem woman. McCoy also fit in with Elvin Jones's dynamic, dense, innovative polyrhythms and Jimmy Garrison's loud, pulsating bass.

McCoy played for the group's first record, *My Favorite Things*, for which Coltrane, originally a tenor player, used soprano saxophone. On the title tune, the chanting style and waltz rhythm added to the exotic sound of the soprano's high register. And Coltrane's modal approach to improvising hypnotized and haunted audiences. With this album, Coltrane established his distinctive sound and style. He and his group vaulted to the top echelons of exciting, inspiring jazz musicians. Coltrane said he loved McCoy's melodic inventiveness, clear ideas, ability to build a structure for a song, and his bright sound and good taste.

Next came Coltrane's albums *Live at the Village Vanguard*, *Impressions*, and *A Love Supreme*. He was playing very heartfelt music. Not only was Coltrane reading a great deal of spiritual literature, but he was deeply affected by the bombing of a church in Alabama in 1963—three children died there during a crusade for integration. Then an alto saxophonist and flutist who had joined Coltrane's group for a while died young from the complications of diabetes. *A Love Supreme* reflected the spirituality that completely overtook Coltrane at this time and helped him rise above his shocks and losses. Playing in Coltrane's group, Tyner, developing as a lyrical, richly modal player, became completely identified with the most important jazz improviser since Charlie Parker. McCoy recorded some albums of his own in these years. But his most important work was done with Coltrane.

In 1965, McCoy decided to leave the group for two reasons. Coltrane was now using two drummers, and McCoy couldn't hear what he was playing on the piano. Furthermore, he wanted to separate from Coltrane and assert his own personality as a leader. For several years, McCoy struggled. Times were so lean for him that some people thought he had quit playing. But by the 1970s, he began to emerge. His problem hadn't been simply that he wasn't playing with the famous Coltrane; in the late

Striders to Beboppers and Beyond

1960s, fusion jazz and rock eclipsed jazz nearly completely. Few acoustic jazz players could earn a living. McCoy refused to play the electric piano or synthesizers, so it took a while for his persistence to pay off.

Building on his earlier ideas of long lines and a heavy sound, his playing became more dense, with a chant-like style. He added African-style percussion to his group and played dazzling, swirling solos while including the swinging tradition in his sound. His music so completely engulfed audiences that critics called it "sheets of sound." (The phrase had originated with critic Ira Gitler, writing about saxophonist John Coltrane.)

McCoy's early rhythm and blues experience may also have shaped his rapturous, enveloping style. From his right hand came a whirl of trills, flourishes, and rhythms, contrasted with blocks of thunderous chords and accents of brief, light phrases from his left hand. On virtually every song he played, he had a heavy-handed style. He could accompany another player mutedly and artfully, and he could sustain a soft and mellow mood for a while. But with his block chords as a foundation, he eventually built songs into monumental edifices of music. Young pianists were in awe of his tidal wave of sound. When he was asked to comment on his love affair with a percussive sound, McCoy answered, "I'm really a drummer."[3]

CHAPTER EIGHT
Cecil Taylor and the Avant Garde

In the jazz world, there were mavericks who didn't fit neatly into the piano legacy. Their goal was to pull apart all the traditions that had been carefully organized and constructed. Their music sounded like the experiments of modern European composers, who were committed to turning their musical heritage inside out and upside down. In the jazz world, people who pulled things apart—the avant garde, or free players, or iconoclasts—constituted a small group. In the 1960s, their atonal, often screeching, pounding, chaotic sounds drove people out of the jazz clubs. Soon the avant garde were playing primarily for themselves, usually without pay in private lofts.

The best-known avant garde pianist is a wiry, enigmatic man named Cecil Taylor. Born on March 15, 1933, he was brought up in a middle-class, African-American neighborhood in Corona, Queens. As a child he studied classical piano and practiced all the time, while his friends played stickball.

Cecil's early tastes in music were traditional. He liked the swing-era bands led by drummers Chick Webb and Gene Krupa. Fascinated with percussion, he studied drums. Later on he would emphasize the percussive properties of the piano. But from the beginning of his career, he also loved Duke Ellington, a master of harmony if there ever was one. Cecil also appreciated the dreaminess and lushness of the harmonies of the modern French Impressionist composer Claude Debussy.

After high school, Cecil went to study classical piano at the New England Conservatory of Music in Boston, where he was attracted to the shocking, modern, atonal European composers Igor Stravinsky, Béla Bartók, Arnold Schoenberg, Alban Berg, and Anton von Webern. All of them had difficulty finding acceptance with mass audiences for their weird sounds. Cecil still found much to love in jazz piano history. The passion and intensity of Bud Powell surfaced in Cecil's work. But he began to take aspects of the old jazz masters—quotes from jazz classics, for example—and pull them apart.

By the late 1950s and early 1960s, Taylor's lone voyage into atonal, wild, avant garde music shocked the jazz world. His runs along the keyboard were an avalanche of notes. Sometimes he pounded the keys with his elbows. He plucked strings. He played a note or two continuously for fifteen minutes, at moments suggesting that he was going to veer off the note and relieve the tension by playing at least one other note. But he turned out to be teasing, and he continued playing the single note. At first, many people, including jazz critics, were upset. They didn't think he was playing jazz, and they questioned whether it was music at all.

He was playing sounds that were a result, a consequence, of jazz. For example, his single, sustained note could be called an exploration of a tone. In that way, he was experimenting with a portion of a mode, which was a series of notes within a scale. He took the idea of tonal exploration to an extreme. He analyzed everything that had been played by the masters and then pulled it apart, or reduced it, or played the opposite. When

120

he began leading his own groups in the 1950s, he didn't accompany other instruments so much as he had dialogues, or even arguments, with them. The agile, resilient pianist broke with every idea that had guided the innovators of jazz piano. By doing so, he turned himself into a remarkable innovator himself. As they began to understand and accept him, critics decided to call him a "free jazz" player.[1]

Fans for his music remained few. Occasionally he worked in clubs or performed concerts in the United States. But he ran into trouble with audiences. In one club, he was fired after one set. Famous jazz musicians, including Miles Davis, walked out of Cecil's performances. Cecil went to Europe, where he found greater acceptance, and he made recordings there. In post-war Berlin, his brand of expressionism found kindred souls among the people who lived in a fractured city. Berlin was divided for decades by a politically motivated, heavily fortified, much-hated wall. Berliners, who lived in a city at war with itself, understood the feelings communicated by Taylor's music.

Serious jazz critics and some musicians increasingly applauded his aims, accepting him as a fresh voice and an innovator in jazz. Ordinary audiences still found his music difficult to love, but in public performances he could be very entertaining. In 1984, for a concert at Carnegie Hall, Oscar Peterson played solo to a cheering audience for the first half of a program. After intermission, Cecil Taylor took over. He was heard emitting cries backstage before he came on stage. Then he entered, emerging from under the piano. He wore a white costume resembling the loincloth adopted by the great Indian spiritual and political leader Mahatma Gandhi. Chanting, Taylor sat down at the piano and began pounding out tone clusters with his entire forearm. (He once said in an interview that he tried to "imitate on the piano the leaps in space a dancer makes."[2]) The audience was divided. About half the people got up and walked out in a steady stream. The other half stayed and happily applauded.

On his albums, he has sounded the same as he does in concerts. His compact disc *In Florescence* on the A&M label, for example, begins with a cry. A few pretty phrases flutter by. Then he moves into his characteristic, thunderous rolls, chants, poetry, and effects varying from the sparest touch of the strings inside the piano to exploding clusters of keys. To appreciate his work, a listener must be adventurous and open-minded about explorations in sound. Music has the power to soothe the savage beast; Cecil has proved that music can also imitate that beast.

A recipient of the so-called "genius" award, the MacArthur Award of about $300,000, Cecil produced and performed in a concert at Lincoln Center in 1994, which the audience loved. He later played for a week at the Village Vanguard, normally a club that must consider the commercial appeal of the musicians it books. And as controversy itself became a persistent part of American society in the 1990s, Cecil Taylor found wider acceptance. He was asked why he developed the way he did. Wearing dreadlocks, sipping champagne, surrounded by a coterie of admirers in a New York jazz club where he was listening to another pianist, he politely and good-naturedly said, "I'm still trying to figure that out myself."[3]

He has influenced other musicians to varying degrees. Among the little group of respected free jazz pianists, Joanne Brackeen holds Cecil Taylor in high esteem. Born in Ventura, California on July 26, 1938, she taught herself to play jazz by listening to mainstream, swing-era jazz pianists on records; by the late 1950s, she was playing in jazz groups in Los Angeles and went on to join distinguished groups led by Art Blakey, Joe Henderson, and Stan Getz.

Whenever she got the chance, she composed free jazz, often ominous, rolling, and low-voiced compositions, experimental music at the fringe of atonality. She could also sound lush and jubilant, or airy, ethereal, and tremulous. She could even play complex Brazilian samba and bossa nova rhythms with authenticity. No one ever was lulled by Joanne's assertive performances, which could always charm, or make merry, or puzzle and shock audiences. Sometimes club owners told her not to play her avant garde music and stay with the standards. She did it reluctantly. But a relentless pioneer, she usually put a little of her unusual sounds into the standards.

By the 1990s, Joanne began to sound more mellow in general as a composer. A new album of her free jazz, *Where Legends Dwell*, had a touch of pensiveness—a laid-back quality balancing the intimations of storminess that had often made her earlier music sound fierce. In one week in 1992, she entertained an audience at the Knickerbocker restaurant— where mainstream jazz is popular—with pretty standards ending with forceful ruminations in the bass register of the piano. The next week, she moved to a jazz club, Visiones, where she led a quartet in relentlessly exciting music that avoided truly shocking harmonies but still explored the fringes of atonality.

Like many free jazz and experimental players, she had mellowed over the years. She seemed to feel most comfortable—and the public liked it best—when she moved back and forth between avant garde and mainstream, commercial jazz. Her music in any style sounded rich and warm, probably because of her experiences with a variety of styles. In the 1990s, she ventured wholeheartedly into Brazilian music; her albums *Breath of Brazil* and *Take a Chance* are romantic, exuberant music. She plays with confidence and courage.

A younger pianist, Don Pullen, born on Christmas Day, 1944 in Roanoke, Virginia, began experimenting with atonality after he heard records by Ornette Coleman. Pullen had a thorough background in gospel and blues, which would always affect his approach to music. Visiting Chicago, he met another experimenter, pianist Muhal Richard Abrams, who encouraged Don to keep trying to incorporate atonality into the standard forms—the blues, popular songs, and jazz standards.

By 1965, Don was immersed in New York's avant garde milieu, a small, fringe group of musicians who recorded on the ESP label. Don thought their music was energetic and vital and reflected the revolutionary, tumultuous times they lived in. Other avant-gardists criticized him for playing riffs that called to mind his gospel and blues background. But he didn't change his ideas. "It's a great attribute of jazz to allow you to play your own history. So I pleased myself, not others," he said.[4]

Striders to Beboppers and Beyond

To survive financially in the 1970s, he played organ in Harlem and Queens clubs; organ music was trendy in those days. He also accompanied well-known jazz and blues singers. A Detroit-born drummer, Roy Brooks, recommended Pullen to Charles Mingus, an experimental bassist and composer, who auditioned and hired Don in 1973. Without a rehearsal, Pullen sight-read Mingus's music in a quintet performance. A very quirky man, Mingus suddenly left the bandstand for twenty minutes. Pullen had to hold his own with the rest of the group. It was a trial by fire, and he survived. He played with Mingus for three years, flourishing in that experimental, musical environment.

He brought his friend, saxophonist George Adams, into the band. Eventually Don and George co-led an exciting quartet of their own. But their drummer died early in 1989. The group played its last date at the Mt. Fuji Festival in Japan. Pullen decided to strike out on his own. At Mt. Fuji, he asked some Blue Note record label executives if he could record with his own trio. That would be fine, they said.

Pullen invited the excellent bassist Gary Peacock and drummer Tony Williams, who had graced one of Miles Davis's groups, to join him. And in 1989, Pullen's album *New Beginnings* aired on the jazz radio stations. Modern jazz fans loved it. It was a jubilant, triumphant blend of all the styles in jazz history, including free jazz. In the music, Don constantly set up horrific crises and resolved them. Playing with fiery, visceral, romantic appeal, he imbued his voyages into atonality with musicality. That requisite for beauty was too often missing from the works of other free jazz players on any instrument.

Played loudly, *New Beginnings* made listeners feel they were negotiating their way, piloted by Pullen, through the white waters of contemporary life. That trip was sometimes exhilarating, sometimes alarming. Then they arrived at a safe haven. The last track of the album, "Silence = Death," a piano solo by Pullen, heightened the pacific melodiousness implied in the first song on the album, "Jana's Happiness," written for his close friend.

More albums followed. He began exploring Latin music with at least seven types of percussion, including an exotic, deep-voiced, primitive, stringed gourd, the Brazilian berimbau. On piano, he could move quickly from dissonant, melodious, subtly shocking and attention-getting rolls to an ethereal sound as shimmering as a harp. If people wanted to, they could have danced to his music. Because his group played such happy sounds, he became the person who would have seemed like an impossible dream in the 1960s—a popular avant-gardist.

"I don't think there's one particular thing that causes development," he said about his attraction to percussion and his evolution to popularity. "Over a period of time, I developed a concept and started to hear my own music. For me, it was a problem of how to get it out. From that came my technique, a rolling-the-palm thing, using the back of the hands, the knuckles. It seemed to be the easiest way for me to get the sounds that I was hearing [inside my head]. And my touch on the piano and my awareness of the potential of the piano developed."[5]

He made several more albums in the 1990s. His appearance at Sweet Basil, a leading jazz club in New York, in the early summer of 1994 brought a crowd of American and African drummers out to hear him. Unfortunately, by that time, Pullen was suffering from lymphoma, a type of cancer. He kept shuttling back and forth between the piano bench and the hospital. But when he was on the bench, audiences were treated to high energy music that would have exhausted healthy young pianists. Don seemed overjoyed. "This is happy music,"[6] commented one admiring drummer listening to Pullen. That seemed to be part of the explanation for Pullen's hardiness. But after a two year battle, Pullen was depleted. He died in April 1995.

Over time, most traditional pianists learned to feel respect for the pioneering corps of free jazz players. Some mainstream players incorporated free jazz ideas into their work. The mainstream began to widen, expanding its banks and enriching itself. Marian McPartland used a blues written by free jazz saxophonist Ornette Coleman for one of her albums. She stated proudly that she felt, in the 1990s, she could play a free jazz piece with the best of them. Her radio show's theme song, a whirling riff, sounds like a free jazz piece.

At the same time that free jazz was gaining greater acceptance, most free jazz pianists—Richie Beirach, Paul Bley, Michele Rosewoman, and Keith Jarrett, to name a few—have mellowed over the years. They began to sound warmer, and they polished and gained control over their experiments to the degree that they could charm some audiences who normally preferred mainstream music. Audiences became more accepting of new sounds. Only Cecil Taylor persisted at the outer edge of the free jazz galaxy.

By the 1990s, a generation of free jazz players began to emerge. They often played at a downtown New York club called the Knitting Factory. It had been started in the 1980s as a showcase for experimental jazz and related music. The newcomers intrigued critics and attracted fiercely loyal little groups of fans. Their music was now usually referred to as "new music."

CHAPTER NINE
A Lost Generation of Jazz PiaNists is FouND

Miraculously, the fragmentation of jazz into many styles didn't destroy the art, even though, in the 1960s and early 1970s, rock's popularity made it seem as if jazz had no future. In 1965, Birdland, the legendary club that had called itself the jazz corner of the world, closed its doors forever. Jazz musicians on all the acoustic instruments began leaving New York. They headed for Europe or for California studios; rock musicians, who played high-decibel music with a simple beat, took over most of the work. Whether mainstream or experimental, jazz musicians had few high-profile clubs in which they could play in New York or any other American city.

For a short time in the late 1960s and early 1970s, rhythm and blues had a great vogue. Folk music festivals, popular since the late 1950s and early 1960s, attracted fans. Rock concerts became overwhelmingly popular, until they grew dangerous. Fights broke out, and people started to avoid them. Along came disco music. People wanted to dance wildly. Then, looking for something new, kids turned to videos, while older people, who were rock fans in the 1960s and early 1970s, started to search for more sophisticated entertainment.

Record companies had vaults filled with jazz recordings. Always trying to make a profit, executives decided to gamble and fill the void left by rock in the entertainment world. The companies reissued old jazz classics. And the businessmen were delighted to see that people bought the old music. At the same time, a new generation of jazz musicians was coming along. The youngsters were very accomplished, for they had been learning their craft and techniques in music schools.

Quietly, all during the reign of rock, jazz had been developing a new lease on life because of changes in society. The National Endowment for the Arts had begun giving grants to jazz musicians. Congress passed equal opportunity laws which prompted music schools to start outreach programs. They recruited talented young jazz musicians to go into the schools. Veteran jazz musicians found jobs teaching on the faculties of those schools.

In New Orleans, a pianist named Ellis Marsalis taught the city's musically gifted youngsters at the New Orleans Center for the Arts. He sent his trumpet-playing son, Wynton, north to a music festival in Massachusetts. There, Gunther Schuller, an influential musician, critic, and educator, heard Wynton and guided him to matriculate at the Juilliard music school. While studying classical music, Wynton played with Art Blakey's Jazz Messengers. Schuller also introduced Wynton to Columbia Records executives. A handsome, soft-spoken, clean-cut youngster with fashionable wire-rimmed glasses, Wynton was offered a contract to record both jazz and classical music.

The contract represented a new gamble for Columbia. They wanted to see if people buying old jazz would also accept a new jazz star. And everyone was surprised. The teenager, with a powerful technique and a haunting sound derived from Miles Davis, became a hit. Young women—white and black—studied his posters, declared him adorable, bought his records, and went to his concerts. Other record companies started looking around for more young Wyntons on all the instruments. Wynton and his family of talented musicians began guiding other gifted musicians to record companies. The Marsalis family became an influential dynasty in jazz.

The established, older players were finding more jobs, too. New jazz clubs opened, and restaurants added jazz to their schedules. Veteran players hired youngsters, and the public got a chance to know about their talents.

Technology played a part in the renewed interest in jazz. Compact discs were introduced in the 1980s, and the public loved them. Yuppies—young, upwardly mobile professional people—liked to show off by owning the latest technology. It proved they were successful and living the good life. They bought jazz on compact discs without knowing they were buying jazz. They had to be told it was jazz, and they liked it.

In 1969, Bradley Cunningham, a lover of jazz piano, had decided to open his own "jazz saloon," as he called it —a small, intimate room with a bar, dining tables, and a space for an upright jazz piano and a bass. He began hiring jazz pianists, many of them famous—Bill Evans, Hank Jones, and Jimmy Rowles among them. Soon Bradley inherited a grand piano from saxophonist Paul Desmond.

Bradley's piano-bass duo room in Greenwich Village caught on with the public. In faraway cities, aspiring jazz pianists talked to each other about their dreams of playing at Bradley's. Other clubs copied Bradley's. And the music world in general nurtured a renaissance of interest in jazz. More jazz clubs opened. Jazz concerts were produced everywhere. Jazz was used for movie soundtracks, commercials, movies, and public events.

Bradley himself died in the late 1980s. His club, even without his great management and vision, continued to be a showcase for hundreds of young pianists and established older masters, some of whom became headlining performers in concerts, festivals, and on recordings.

Striders to Beboppers and Beyond

The resurgence of public interest in jazz made life easier for the remaining grand old masters. The Modern Jazz Quartet, which had disbanded, started working together again, with John Lewis still at the piano. In the 1980s, Earl Hines and Teddy Wilson became celebrated again. Musicians who had retired came out to star in jazz and supper clubs. Dorothy Donegan, who had been touring in Europe and hadn't played in New York in years, suddenly surfaced in a Kool Jazz Festival concert in 1980. John S. Wilson, a knowledgeable, tasteful critic for the *New York Times* praised her "subliminal sense of swing"[1] in a dazzling performance, adding that she had been sorely missed on the New York jazz scene.

A middle generation of journeyman pianists—McCoy Tyner's contemporaries and slightly younger musicians, such as Cedar Walton, Kirk Lightsey, John Hicks, Bill Mays, Roger Kellaway, to name a few—also found themselves in greater demand. They had survived in the 1960s and 1970s by working in the studios, playing the blues, composing for television, or just depending on their wits.

And from the younger generation came a new master, Kenny Barron. He was born in Philadelphia on July 9, 1943, but had been living in New York City since the early 1960s. His older brother, Bill, a saxophonist, had helped make the early days in New York easier for Kenny. Living near his brother on the Lower East Side of Manhattan in a community of jazz musicians, Kenny found little jobs in clubs, coffee shops, and bars. He played with saxophonist James Moody, drummer Roy Haynes, and Dizzy Gillespie. Kenny and his brother occasionally played in a group at Birdland. Around the corner from his apartment house were well-known clubs, the Five Spot and the Jazz Gallery, where Kenny heard Cecil Taylor play.

With his wife, whom he had met in high school, Kenny moved to Brooklyn, which also had several clubs and a community of jazz musicians. And he was on the New York scene when saxophonist Ornette Coleman blew into town with his controversial new music. Working in a group led by trumpeter Freddie Hubbard in the late 1960s, Kenny played

130

a great deal of avant garde music. "It was especially difficult to work in those days, if you didn't play that kind of music," Kenny reminisced.[2] But the styles of music he played never changed his mind about his original aesthetic goals. He wanted to play artistically beautiful, modern mainstream jazz that encompassed the history of jazz piano's development.

Kenny played exciting music throughout the 1960s as a meticulous, bebop-rooted pianist. He then became one of the primary soloists with bassist Ron Carter's group in the mid-1970s. Carter had starred in one of Miles Davis's most important groups. Then Kenny joined forces with three other musicians from Carter's group to establish a quartet called Sphere. In the 1980s, it won high praise for its smooth, modern music. The musicians wanted to play their own compositions as well as the best of the jazz repertory. All of the songs on their last album, *Bird Songs*, on Verve, were written by Kenny.

"Sphere was a fantastic experience in more ways than one," Kenny said. "It showed us what we could do with determination. The first two Sphere records we paid for ourselves. We spent a lot of money, down to the details of the photographs. And it worked. It required a certain amount of sacrifice, and we all did it."[3] As an equal partner in that collective group, Kenny put the finishing touches on his playing. The responsibility for cooperative leadership enhanced his self-confidence and made him feel free to express himself more and more. With Sphere playing his compositions, his creative imagination gained momentum. The standards he set for his performances elevated them to the innovative. There was no mood, technique, or idea beyond his musical grasp. Unfortunately, the quartet's saxophonist, Charlie Rouse, who had become prominent working with Thelonious Monk years earlier, died of cancer. Heartbroken, Sphere's remaining members broke up the group.

But opportunities for Kenny to widen his horizons kept coming. Invited to record with several excellent European-born musicians, he was critically praised for his work. He started leading his own groups—quintets and trios—in clubs and on albums. He hired the bassist and drummer from Sphere for some of those groups. And he aspired to lead his groups the way Miles Davis had done, letting the musicians do whatever they wanted to as soloists.

In the 1980s, he received two NEA grants for study and performance. He ranked third as a pianist, for the first time in his life, in the *Down Beat* International Critics Poll. "I had been in the polls only once before, in the category of Talent Deserving Wider Recognition," he recalled, somewhat mystified and amused by his selection as a player of electric piano, an instrument he rarely used.[4]

Early in his career, Kenny was following in his brother Bill's footsteps as a teacher. In 1972, he found a job teaching in the Jazzmobile Workshop, a school for jazz study based in Harlem. The next year, he became an instructor at Rutgers University's Livingston College in New Jersey. The school had a fledgling jazz faculty which grew to offer bachelor and master of music degrees. As the jazz program grew, Kenny became a full, tenured professor. He had the luxury and responsibility of staying home and raising his family on a secure income.

As a performer, with long flowing lines, a clear, articulate touch, and flawless creative ideas for embellishments, improvisation, and compositions, Kenny began to assert himself as one of the greatest jazz piano players. Many people who went to hear pianists often considered him to be the best living jazz pianist—even better than the modern masters of technique and harmonies, Tommy Flanagan and Hank Jones. Whenever Kenny played in a club in New York, crowds showed up. He signed a contract with a big recording company, Verve/Gitanes, based in Paris, in the 1990s.

One night, quite late, in a New York club, Kenny enthralled the crowd with his exuberant performance of "Manha de Carneval—A Day in the Life of a Fool," a Brazilian song from the movie *Black Orpheus*. As usual, his long, flowing lines combined a delicate balance of ease and tension. As the music swelled with romantic, hedonistic feeling, Kenny suddenly chose a weirdly dissonant chord. Everyone looked up, startled, and laughed. He played a few more zany, glaring dissonances to make the song unforgettable and interesting. Every time he sat down to play, he made it clear that he could play anything musically possible on a keyboard.

A Lost Generation of Jazz Pianists is Found

As he was putting the finishing touches on his reputation, inheriting the mantle from the greatest players in jazz history, along came a new generation of pianists. They were filled with energy, ideas, and dreams of fame, fortune, and self-expression with their own compositions. Many had spellbinding techniques they had learned, for the most part, in music colleges and conservatories. They were well-versed in the history of jazz. And they chose to go in one of two ways: either to the mainstream or to the avant garde. Those who joined the mainstream started to get a great deal of exposure in the flourishing jazz world. Recording contracts from major companies became available to some of them.

They were regarded as neoclassicists, both for playing the old repertoire and for writing their own compositions, with greater or lesser success, in traditional styles. The pianists came to New York from all over the world—from Canada, Detroit, Mississippi, the West Coast, Europe, small towns all over the United States, even Asia, Africa, South America, the Caribbean, and the West Indies. Intensely committed, driving themselves to compete in the crowded jazz scene headquartered in New York, many of them worked their way to center stage at Carnegie Hall and Lincoln Center. The press paid attention to them, and in interviews they said they were challenging themselves to become better players, more successful group leaders, and greater composers.

In 1991, when someone asked tall, courtly Mulgrew Miller, a Mississippi-born pianist who had worked with the Ellington band and won great praise in New York City since the 1980s, if he didn't already have exorbitant control, he agreed that he had a great deal. "But I think I can do it more completely," he said.[5] He wanted to develop his career as a leader.

For a while, Mulgrew worked in a prominent drummer's band, then left it and committed himself to his own group for recordings and tours. "I'm taking things from day to day," he said softly in his seemingly relaxed way.[6] But like all the young, virtuosic leaders, he was faced with the intense pressures of finding bookings and proper personnel and of earning profits for club owners and record producers. A college-educated, accomplished, and spiritually searching musician, Mulgrew belonged to a generation of jazz players who functioned as serious, struggling artists in their private practice spaces and then walked out onto glamorous stages and bandstands to conduct high-pressured, well-illuminated careers. They played for big financial stakes as well as for their goals of artistic perfection.

Among the hundreds of new artists who followed Mulgrew came Geri Allen, Renee Rosnes, Benny Green, Marcus Roberts, Kenny Kirkland, Billy Childs, Niels Lan Doky, Kenny Drew Jr., Stephen Scott, Diana Krall, Rachel Z, Cyrus Chestnut, and Danilo Perez, to name just a few of the new piano stars. All of them had first committed themselves to a search for the right group leaders to hire them and the right recording contracts to show them off. Those goals accomplished, the young artists went on to search for the right manager, the right bookings, the best songs and arrangements and side people for their groups—the best of everything.

They face so many musical challenges and so much competition. Younger pianists keep coming along all the time. Record companies are always looking for the youngest possible players to promote as new stars. Only one thing is certain in the complex lives of the neoclassicists: With so much jazz piano history behind them, so much artistry at their command, and so much public interest in jazz piano music, it is a fine time to be a jazz pianist.

Source Notes

Introduction

1 This description coined by Ira Gitler. Also found in *Jazz Styles: History and Analysis*, fifth edition, by Mark C. Gridley (Englewood Cliffs, N.J.: Prentice Hall, 1994), p. 253.

2 *Jazz Piano*, Smithsonian Collection of Recordings (Washington, D.C.: Smithsonian Press, 1989), p. 21.

Chapter One

1 Len Lyons, *The Great Jazz Pianists* (New York: Quill, William Morrow and Company, 1983), p. 21.

2 Marshall W. Stearns, *The Story of Jazz* (New York: Oxford University Press, 1970), p. 63. (Here called "Creoles of Color," interchangeable with "People of Color" cited in many history books.)

3 Alan Lomax, *Mister Jelly Roll* (New York: Pantheon Books, 1978), p. 30.

4 Interview by author with singer Joe Williams, mid-1980s. Williams has used this anecdote many times in performances.

5 Joel Vance, *Fats Waller: His Life and Times* (London: Robson Books, 1979), p. 31.

6 Ibid., p. 111.

7 Leslie Gourse, "Joe Turner: An American Stride Pianist in Paris," *Contemporary Keyboard* (August 1980), pp. 20–21. All subsequent quotations from Turner come from the same source, an interview conducted in Paris.

8 Stearns, p. 12.

9 Barry Singer, *Black and Blue: The Life and Lyrics of Andy Razaf* (New York: Schirmer Books, 1992), p. 110.

10 Ibid., p. 119.

11 Vance, p. 111.

12 Rex Stewart, *Jazz Masters of the 30s* (New York: Da Capo Books, 1985), p. 187.

13 Interview by author with pianist Cyrus Chestnut, 1995.

Chapter Two

1 Marshall W. Stearns, *The Story of Jazz* (New York: Oxford University Press, 1970), p. 107.

2 George T. Simon, *The Big Bands* (New York:

Schirmer Books, 1981), pp. 54–63.

3 Stearns, p. 167.

4 Stanley Dance, *The World of Earl Hines* (New York: Da Capo Books, 1977), p. 9.

5 Ibid., p. 10.

6 Ibid., p. 16.

7 Ibid., p. 18.

8 Ibid., p. 20.

9 Ibid., p. 42.

10 Ibid., p. 45.

11 Ibid., p. 47.

12 Ibid., p. 62.

13 Leslie Gourse, "Jay McShann, Confessin' the Blues," *Kansas City* magazine (January 1982), pp. 44–45.

14 Leslie Gourse, *Unforgettable: The Life and Mystique of Nat King Cole* (New York: St. Martin's Press, 1991), p. 8.

15 Len Lyons, *The Great Jazz Pianists* (New York: Quill, William Morrow and Company, 1983), p. 27.

16 Ibid., p. 31.

17 Gourse, "Jay McShann, Confessin' the Blues." All subsequent quotations from Jay McShann come from this source.

18 Dance, p. 184.

19 Lyons, *The Great Jazz Pianists*, p. 61.

20 *Piano Jazz*, with Marian McPartland, host, and Teddy Wilson, Jazz Alliance compact disc TJA-12002.

21 Linda Dahl, *Stormy Weather: The Music and Lives of a Century of Jazzwomen* (New York: Pantheon Books, 1984), p. 61.

22 Liner notes from *The Zodiac Suite*, with Mary Lou Williams, pianist and composer, in concert at Town Hall, New York, December 31, 1945, Vintage Jazz Classics compact disc VJC-1035.

23 Ibid.

24 Dahl, p. 62.

25 Liner notes from *The Zodiac Suite*.

26 Interview by author with drummer Gerard Pochenet, New York, mid-1980s.

27 Ibid.

28 Interview by author with singer Thelma Carpenter, New York, mid-1980s.

29 Interview with Gerard Pochenet.

30 Leslie Gourse, *Madame Jazz: Contemporary Women Instrumentalists* (New York: Oxford University Press, 1995), p. 37.

Chapter Three

1 Len Lyons, *The Great Jazz Pianists* (New York: Quill, William Morrow and Company, 1983), p. 96.

2 Leslie Gourse, *Madame Jazz: Contemporary Women Instrumentalists* (New York: Oxford University Press, 1995), p. 192.

3 Interview by author with Toshiko Akiyoshi, early 1980s.

Chapter Four

1 Dizzy Gillespie with Al Fraser, *To Be Or Not To Bop* (Garden City, N.Y.: Doubleday and Company, 1979), p. 144.

2 Ibid., p. 252.

3 Ira Gitler, *Swing To Bop* (New York: Oxford University Press, 1985), p. 121.

4 Gillespie and Fraser, p. 337.

5 Liner notes by Orrin Keepnews for *Thelonious Monk: The Complete Riverside Recordings*, a boxed collection of reissued LPs, Fantasy Records, Inc., 1986.

6 Ibid.

7 Interview by author with Thelonious Sphere Monk Jr.

8 Max Gordon, *Live from the Village Vanguard* (New York: Da Capo Books, 1986), p. 120.

9 Interview by author with Thelonious Sphere Monk Jr.

10 Bill Crow, *Jazz Anecdotes* (New York: Oxford University Press, 1990), p. 45.

11 Liner notes by Max Harrison for "Presto Serioso," on *The Best of Bud Powell on Verve*, Verve compact disc 314-523-392-2 (1994).

12 Gitler, p. 120.

13 Ibid., p. 121.

14 Ibid., p. 112

15 Ibid., p. 113.

16 Gary Giddins, "Strictly Confidential," *Village Voice*, Jazz Special (June 28, 1994), p. 3.

17 Gitler, p. 128.

18 Interview by author with pianist Bertha Hope.

Chapter Six

1 Probably Max Jones, critic, in the British music magazine *The Melody Maker*. The term came into general usage when referring to Miles Davis's sound.

2 Marian McPartland quoted in "A Closing Note on Bill Evans" by Richard M. Sudhalter, *New York Post*, September 18, 1980.

3 Interview by author with drummer Jimmy Cobb, 1995.

4 Ibid.

5 Leslie Gourse, "Herbie Hancock: Oscar Brings New High Point to Pianist's Career," *Ebony Man* (September 1987), pp. 42, 46. All quotations from Herbie Hancock come from this source.

6 Lyons, *101 Best Jazz Albums: A History of Jazz on Records* (New York: Quill, William Morrow and Company, 1980), p. 353.

7 Ibid., p. 354.

8 Ibid.

9 Ibid., p. 356.

Chapter Seven

1 J. B. Alexander, "McCoy Tyner Comes Out of the Shadows," *New York Post*, January 20, 1976.

2 Ibid.

3 McCoy Tyner in conversation with Leslie Gourse, in Sweet Basil, a jazz club, New York City, 1993.

Chapter Eight

1 Lyons, *101 Best Jazz Albums: A History of Jazz on Records* (New York: Quill, William Morrow and Company, 1980), p. 393.

2 Ibid., p. 399.

3 Leslie Gourse, article on the Loud and Percussive Jazz Pianists, *Jazz Iz* magazine (August–September 1992), p. 93.

4 Leslie Gourse, "Don Pullen," *Jazz Times* (November 1989), p. 21.

5 Leslie Gourse, article on the Loud and Percussive Jazz Pianists, p. 91.

6 Drummer Pheeroan Aklaff commenting on Don Pullen's performance at Sweet Basil, New York City, summer 1994.

Chapter Nine

1 John S. Wilson, *New York Times*, June 1980.

2 Leslie Gourse, "Kenny Barron: anything musically possible," *Jazz Times* (January 1989), p. 13.

3 Ibid.

4 Ibid., p. 20.

5 Leslie Gourse, "Mulgrew Miller," *Jazz Times* (January–February 1991), p. 26.

6 Ibid.

Suggested Listening

Here's a variety of compact discs. Not everything will be available at all times in stores, but there will always be reasonable alternatives. Music departments of libraries have many CDs, too.

An exciting collection of the styles of many innovators and virtuosos has been compiled by The Smithsonian Collection of Recordings, a division of Smithsonian Institution Press, Washington, D.C. 20560. Titled *Jazz Piano*, it includes Jelly Roll Morton, James P. Johnson, Willie "the Lion" Smith, Fats Waller, Earl Hines, Teddy Wilson, Jimmy Yancey, Meade "Lux" Lewis, Pete Johnson, Avery Parrish with Erskine Hawkins, Count Basie, Billy Kyle, Mary Lou Williams, Art Tatum, Duke Ellington, Jess Stacy, Nat "King" Cole, Erroll Garner, Jimmy Jones, Bud Powell, Lennie Tristano, Dodo Marmarosa, Ellis Larkins, Dave McKenna, Al Haig, Oscar Peterson, Jimmy Rowles, Thelonious Monk, Phineas Newborn Jr., Horace Silver, Martial Solal, Herbie Nichols, Hank Jones, Tommy Flanagan, Hank Jones, John Lewis, Randy Weston, Ray Bryant, Bill Evans, McCoy Tyner, Chick Corea, Keith Jarrett, and Herbie Hancock.

Another sampler, from Verve, is simply titled *Piano*. It contains performances by George Wallington, Barry Harris, Bud Powell, John Williams, Paul Bley, Marian McPartland, Beryl Booker, Nat "King" Cole, Teddy Wilson, Bernard Pfiffer, Bill Evans, Hampton Hawes, Junior Mance, and Red Garland.

Other recordings are:

Jelly Roll Morton (1926–1934), ABC Music.

Eubie Blake, *Memories of You—From Rare Piano Rolls*, Biograph, 1990.

James P. Johnson, *Carolina Shout*, Biograph; *Piano Solos*, Folkways-Smithsonian; *Snowy Morning Blues*, Decca, GRP.

Fats Waller, *The Definitive Fats Waller: His Piano His Rhythm*, Stash; *The Joint Is Jumpin'*, RCA Blue Bird.

Earl Hines Plays Duke Ellington, piano solos recorded 1971–1975, New World Records; *Piano Man!*, 1928–1940, Swing Era. Earl Hines, *A Monday Date*,

Original Jazz Classics. Also on Riverside.

Louis Armstrong: Hot Fives and Hot Sevens, Vols. 1 and 2, JSP (imported from England); and *Louis Armstrong: Hot Fives and Sevens*, Vols. 1, 2, and 3, Columbia. Both contain famous Armstrong-Hines collaborations from the 1920s.

Art Tatum, *Masters of Jazz*, Storyville; *Solo Masterpieces*, Vols. 1–8, Pablo; The Best of . . ., Pablo; *The Complete Capitol Recordings* (1949–1952), Vols. 1 and 2, Capitol/EMI; *I Got Rhythm*, Vol. 3, 1935–1944, GRP.

Striders to Beboppers and Beyond

Teddy Wilson, *His Piano and Orchestra*, with Billie Holiday, ASV; *Stomping At the Savoy, Air Mail Special, and Runnin' Wild*, all on Black Lion.

Duke Ellington: The bins are filled with his band's recordings. Among them are *16 Most Requested Songs*, Columbia, released in 1994; *Duke Ellington — The Blanton-Webster Band, 1940–1942*, Bluebird; *Piano Reflections*, piano solos, Capitol, 1953.

Count Basie: The bins are also filled with his band recordings from the 1930s to the 1980s. Among them are *Count Basie Swings, Joe Williams Sings*, Verve; a trio album, *For the Second Time*, with Basie, Ray Brown, and Louis Bellson, Pablo, 1975; *Count Basie — Basie Swing*, 2-CD set, JWD, 1955–1959; *The Best of the Count Basie Orchestra on Decca*, reissued in 1995, and *Count Basie*, both on Verve. Last two both contain his hits "April in Paris" and "One O'Clock Jump."

Marian McPartland, *Personal Choice*, 1983; *In My Life*, 1993; *. . . Plays the Music of Mary Lou Williams*, 1994; all on Concord.

Nat "King" Cole, *The Piano Style of Nat King Cole*, Capitol/EMI, 1955; *Best of the Nat "King" Cole Trio*, Capitol/EMI.

Thelonious Monk/John Coltrane Live at the Five Spot: Discovery!, recorded 1957, issued on Blue Note, 1993. *Thelonious Monk Plays Duke Ellington*, Riverside, 1955; *Brilliant Corners*, Riverside, 1956; *Solo Monk*, Columbia/Legacy, originally recorded 1964–1965, reissued 1992.

Bud Powell, *The Genius of . . .*, Verve, 1950; *Salt Peanuts*, Black Lion, 1964; *Jazz Great*, Verve, 1950; *The Amazing . . .*, Blue Note, 1950–1960; *The Best of . . .*, Blue Note; *The Bud Powell Trio Plays*, Roulette, 1947–1953.

George Shearing, *Nat King Cole Sings, George Shearing Plays*, Capitol/EMI, 1962; *Once Again — That Shearing Sound*, Telarc.

George Shearing Quintet, *On the Sunny Side of the Street*, GRP Crescendo.

Erroll Garner, *Concert By The Sea*, Columbia 1956.

Dorothy Donegan, *Live at the 1990 Floating Jazz Festival*, Chiaroscuro Records, 1991; *Dorothy Romps*, Rosetta Records, 1991.

Dave Brubeck/Paul Desmond, Fantasy, 1952–1954; *Jazz Impressions of Eurasia*, Legacy, 1958.

The Modern Jazz Quartet, *Concorde*, Original Jazz Classics; *Echoes — Together Again*, 1984.

Oscar Peterson, *The Trio*, with Ray Brown and Ed Thigpen, live from Chicago, Verve, 1961; *Time After Time*, Pablo.

Bill Evans, *At The Village Vanguard*, with bassist Scott LaFaro and drummer Paul Motian, Riverside, 1961; *Blue in Green*, with bassist Eddie Gomez, Milestone, 1974; *The Solo Sessions*, Vol. 1, Milestone, 1963.

Hank Jones, *Handful of Keys*, Verve.

Tommy Flanagan, *Lady Be Good*, Verve, 1994; The Tokyo Recital, Original Jazz Classics, 1975.

Bobby Timmons, contains his songs "Moanin'," "This Here," and "Dat Dere," Original Jazz Classics, 1960.

Horace Silver, *The Best of . . . The Blue Note Year*, Vol. 2, Blue Note, 1953–1959.

Chick Corea, *Light as a Feather*, Verve, 1973, and *A.R.C.*, ECM, both with Return to Forever band; *An Evening With Chick Corea and Herbie Hancock*, Polydor, 1978; Chick Corea, *Electric Band*, GRP; *Piano*

Improvisations, Vol. 1, ECM.

Joe Zawinul, *Black Water*, Tristar, and *The Immigrants*, Columbia, both with The Zawinul Syndicate.

Red Garland, *A Garland of Red*, Original Jazz Classics, 1954.

Wynton Kelly, *Piano Interpretations*, Blue Note.

Herbie Hancock, *Maiden Voyage*, 1965; *Speak Like a Child*, 1968; *The Best of . . .*, Vol. 2 (contains "Watermelon Man,"), all on Blue Note. *New Standards*, Verve, 1996.

Keith Jarrett, *The Köln Concert*, ECM, 1975.

McCoy Tyner, on John Coltrane recordings, early 1960s; also *Echoes of a Friend*, Original Jazz Classics, 1977; *Live at Sweet Basil*, with bassist Avery Sharpe, Evidence, 1989.

Kenny Barron, *Scratch*, with Dave Holland and Daniel Humair, Enja; *On Tour*, 1985, and *Pumpkin's Delight*, 1986, both with the group Sphere, Red Records.

Cedar Walton, *Among Friends*, Evidence, 1992; *St. Thomas*, with bassist Ron Carter and drummer Billy Higgins, Sweet Basil Trio, Evidence, 1996.

Kirk Lightsey, *Everything Is Changed*, 1987, and *Lightsey I*, 1983, both on Sunnyside.

John Hicks, *Duality*, with guitarist Peter Leitch, Reservoir, 1995; *Crazy For You*, Red Baron, 1992; *Two of a Kind*, with bassist Ray Drummond, Evidence, 1989.

Mulgrew Miller, *From Day to Day*, 1990, and *Work*, both on Landmark; *With Our Own Eyes*, Novus.

Bill Mays, *An Ellington Affair*, with bassist

John Goldsby and drummer Lewis Nash, Concord, 1995; *One to One*, Vol. 1, with bassist Ray Drummond, DMP, 1990.

The Key Players, the Contemporary Piano Ensemble, with Mulgrew Miller, James Williams, Donald Brown, Harold Mabern, and Geoff Keezer, Columbia/DIW, early 1990s.

Cecil Taylor, *Unit Structures*, Blue Note; *Silent Tongues*, Freedom, 1975.

Joanne Brackeen, *Breath of Brazil*, Concord Picante, 1991; *Where Legends Dwell*, Ken Music.

Don Pullen, *New Beginnings*, Blue Note, 1989.

Geri Allen, *Twenty One*, 1994, and *Maroons*, 1992, both on Blue Note.

Billy Childs, *Take for Example This* and *His April Touch*, both on Windham Hill Jazz.

Jazz Piano Series:

Concord Records has been recording two series, one with jazz pianists in solo concerts, and the other with pianists in duos with bassists or guitarists, and issuing CDs. The series are both called "Live At Maybeck Hall."

Jazz Alliance is issuing *Piano Jazz*, Marian McPartland's radio show, on CDs.

Readers should know that there are at least another thousand jazz pianists who should be included in this book, but it was impossible to mention all of them without confusing the story of the development of the art of jazz piano. Some of them have recorded solo albums in the great "Live at Maybeck Hall" series produced by Concord.

For Further Reading

Hundreds of excellent articles about jazz pianists have been written for music magazines. Back issues can be found in many libraries, and current issues are for sale on newsstands. Generally distributed to newsstands and collected in libraries are *Down Beat, Jazz Times, Jazz Iz,* and *Keyboard*.

Balliett, Whitney. *Jelly Roll, Jabbo and Fats*. New York: Oxford University Press, 1983.

Basie, Count, as told to Albert Murray. *Good Morning Blues: The Autobiography of Count Basie*. New York: Random House, 1985; Da Capo Books, 1985.

Dahl, Linda. *Stormy Weather: The Music and Lives of a Century of Jazzwomen*. New York: Pantheon Books, 1984.

Dance, Stanley. *The World of Duke Ellington*. New York: Da Capo Books, 1980 (paperback reprint; originally published 1970).

Dance, Stanley. *The World of Earl Hines*. New York: Da Capo Books, 1977.

Ellington, Duke. *Music Is My Mistress*. New York: Doubleday, 1973. Several reprints available from Da Capo Books, New York, since 1976.

Feather, Leonard. *From Satchmo to Miles*. New York: Da Capo Books, 1972, 1984.

Giddins, Gary. *Rhythm-A-Ning: Jazz Traditions and Innovation in the '80s*. New York: Oxford University Press, 1986.

Gillespie, Dizzy, with Al Fraser. *To Be Or Not To Bop*. Garden City, N.Y.: Doubleday and Company, 1979.

Gitler, Ira. *Jazz Masters of the '40s*. New York: Macmillan, 1966. Paperback reprint by Da Capo Books, New York, 1983.

Gitler, Ira. *Swing To Bop*. New York: Oxford University Press, 1985.

Goldberg, Joe. *Jazz Masters of the '50s*. New York: Macmillan, 1965. Reprinted by Da Capo Books, New York, 1983.

Gordon, Max. *Live from the Village Vanguard*. New York: Da Capo Books, 1986.

Gourse, Leslie. *Madame Jazz: Contemporary Women Instrumentalists*. New York: Oxford University Press, 1995, paperback 1996.

Gourse, Leslie. *Unforgettable: The Life and Mystique of Nat King Cole*. New York: St. Martin's Press, 1991, paperback 1992.

For Further Reading

Gridley, Mark C. *Jazz Styles: History and Analysis,* fifth edition. Englewood Cliffs, N.J.: Prentice Hall, 1994.

Hajdu, David. *Lush Life.* New York: Farrar, Straus and Giroux, 1996. A biography of pianist, composer, and arranger Billy Strayhorn, who worked closely with Duke Ellington.

Hasse, John Edward. Beyond Category: *The Life and Genius of Duke Ellington.* New York: Simon & Schuster, 1993. Paperback reprint by Da Capo Books, New York, 1995.

Hentoff, Nat. *The Jazz Life.* London: Peter Davies, 1962. Paperback reprint by Da Capo Books, New York, 1975.

Jazz Piano. Smithsonian Collection of Recordings (booklet accompanies recordings). Washington, D.C.: Smithsonian Press, 1989.

Lees, Gene. *Oscar Peterson.* Rocklin, Calif.: Prima Publishing and Communications, 1990.

Lomax, Alan. *Mister Jelly Roll.* New York: Pantheon Books, 1978.

Lyons, Len. *101 Best Jazz Albums: A History of Jazz on Records.* New York: Quill, William Morrow and Company, 1980.

Lyons, Len. *The Great Jazz Pianists.* New York: Quill, William Morrow and Company, 1983; Da Capo Books, 1989.

Simon, George T. *The Big Bands.* New York: Schirmer Books, 1981.

Singer, Barry. *Black and Blue: The Life and Lyrics of Andy Razaf.* New York: Schirmer Books, 1992, paperback 1995.

Spellman, A. B. *Four Lives in the Bebop Business.* (Includes sections on pianists Herbie Nichols and Cecil Taylor.) New York: Limelight Editions, 1985. (Originally published 1966.)

Stearns, Marshall W. *The Story of Jazz.* New York: Oxford University Press, 1970.

Stewart, Rex. *Jazz Masters of the '30s.* New York: Macmillan, 1972. Paperback reprint by Da Capo Books, New York, 1985.

Vance, Joel. *Fats Waller: His Life and Times.* London: Robson Books, 1979.

Williams, Martin. *Jazz In Its Time.* New York: Oxford University Press, 1985.

Williams, Martin. *Jazz Masters in Transition, 1957–1969.* New York: Macmillan, 1970. Reprinted by Da Capo Books, New York, 1980.

Williams, Martin. *The Jazz Tradition.* New York: Oxford University Press, 1970. (Reprinted in later editions, including 1993.)

Index

Page numbers in *italics* refer to photographs. Principal references to musicians appear in **boldface**.